How to Self Publish an Adult Coloring Book on
CreateSpace

By

Jason Hamilton

CONTENTS

PREFACE

In early 2015 adult coloring books made a sudden and dramatic jump to the top of Amazon's best seller's list and they have stayed there, earning hundreds of thousands of dollars for both the artists and publishers. This success started a gold rush in the creation of new coloring books, in no small part aided by Amazon's CreateSpace publishing on demand program. Unlike traditional book printers, CreateSpace allows artists and independent authors to publish books without fear of rejection, editorial control, or, most importantly upfront costs.

I am not a professional artist but drawing was a hobby of mine. When a friend suffered an illness, she asked me to draw a few pictures for her to color. She passed copies to her friends, who suggested I make a coloring book.

I knew nothing about publishing a coloring book, so I turned to Google to research what was involved. There are many resources out there, but few that go beyond the basics of publishing on CreateSpace. I saw nothing that went into enough detail from an artist's perspective, like how to get CreateSpace to print my line art so it isn't fuzzy.

Amazon currently says that 143,950 new books have been released in the last 30 days. A significant portion are coloring books. Your book will compete with well established names, publishers, and artists who are all doing their very best to maximize sales of their own books.

If you want to follow your passion, or cross publishing a book off your bucket list, go for it. It's easy and there are very few rules. But if your goal is to recoup your time, or even have an income (and it is possible to succeed and generate a healthy income with adult coloring books), you need to learn how to develop a product that appeals to the consumer, and how to market it to the people who purchase adult coloring books.

This book is not for beginners who do not have any experience with computers or art. It is not a step by step guide where I hold your hand throughout the entire process. If that is what you need, you may be in over your head and should consider basic computer and graphics software instruction, or make use of the many services, including one by CreateSpace, that will design your publication for a fee.

However, if you have a body of work, or are in the idea stage and you would like to make coloring book through CreateSpace, then I hope the information in this book is instructive and enlightening.

Unrealistic Expectations

As a result of media attention given to coloring book artists who have made hundreds of thousands, if not millions of dollars, many courses and books have sprung up promising to teach anyone how to publish their very own coloring book and get rich quick.

Have you ever wondered about psychics who claim they can tell the future? The obvious question is, if they can see the future why are they putting neon signs in storefronts, buying TV ads, and working the phones when they could just pick the winning lottery numbers?

Go into any bookstore and you'll see a shelf full of books by successful day traders telling you how they made millions on the stock market. If they can make millions as a day trader, why are they wasting their time writing books – and why are they telling you the secrets of how they did it? It is because they used practices that are no longer valid. Now they make money by telling others how they did it – implying that copying their methods will give you the same results.

All the technical information you need to publish a coloring book is freely available on the web. Free software programs will let you create art or manipulate graphics, and CreateSpace provides templates and will walk you through publishing your coloring book with virtually no upfront costs. The adult coloring book genre is so new, we're still discovering what does and does not work when it comes to marketing.

So, if you're laying out money for a class or book that claims it will teach you how to make a coloring book, make sure the instructor is more than an authority on selling their own courses. Make sure they are an authority on creating and marketing successful coloring books too.

If someone is presenting themselves as an expert, it is quite fair for their students to expect specifics that validate their claims. Don't accept vague or unproven statements about their success. Check to be sure they're telling the truth. Do your due diligence. What are the names of the coloring books they have produced? Where are the books sold, and for what price? Amazon owns more than 70% of the online book market and online printed book market, so Amazon Best Sellers Rank (listed under Product Details on the sales page) and sales rank history (which tracks BSR and can be found on PriceZombie.com and Keepa.com) is a good indicator of success.

Beware of courses where the instructor claims their students are successful. You do not know if the student's success is because of their own efforts or the instruction they received. Beware of courses where the instructor claims they do not sell their books on Amazon or anywhere else that cannot be validated, there's a high chance they are fabricating sales information.

About Me

My name is Jason Hamilton. I'm a software engineer for a Fortune 50 company, who has created multiple coloring books in my spare time. I publish via CreateSpace for sale exclusively on Amazon.

My first two coloring books were selling between 80 - 300 books per day within sixty days of publication. I am not a top 100 author, but I was the author of a top 20 CreateSpace coloring book in October, November, and December 2015. I got there by educating myself in creating and marketing a quality product.

You only have to spend a few minutes reading coloring book groups to realize the books we publish are helping ordinary people deal with the stresses of daily life, as well those who suffer with mental and physical illnesses. Besides that, coloring is just plain fun and taps into everyone's creativity.

With Print on Demand (POD), anyone can become an author. I've been watching people throw together coloring books without any knowledge, research, or skill, because they've been told they don't need knowledge, research, or skill to publish a coloring book by "instructors" who lead them on with promises of success if they just pay for their course and follow their advice. Now the market is flooded with thousands of poorly made coloring books that do not sell. The authors can't figure out why.

I created a Facebook group called Coloring Book Author Support, where coloring book authors share information, tips and tricks with each other.

Why should we care if other coloring books are successful? Why would we give away information on how to make a better product and sell more books, to our competition?

Because bad coloring books hurt the entire coloring book market. A buyer who is disappointed in the quality of the content of a recent purchase may well think twice about making another purchase from the same publisher.

As independent CreateSpace authors, we want our buyers to be thrilled with their purchase. We want to attract them with a beautiful cover and impress them with the quality of the artwork on the interior pages. We want them to be confident their money is well spent when they hit the buy button.

My goal is to help the adult coloring book market grow in both size and quality. To that end, this book is about informing new authors how to make a quality coloring book and avoid the common pitfalls.

This will help keep the sales momentum going on coloring books, and help us all be more successful in the long term.

So many coloring books, so few sales...

Unfortunately, the vast majority of coloring books sell only one or two copies per month. We know this by viewing the book's "Best Seller's Rank", or BSR.

While you can certainly sell your coloring books through other venues, as the world's largest book seller, Amazon is vital to your success. Amazon has long commanded 75% of the online market for trade books in print form.

Every product on Amazon has a BSR that rates that product against others in the same category. You can view the best seller's rank on the product page under "Product Details":

Amazon Best Sellers Rank: #4,851 in Books

While there are subcategories nested under the main "Books" category, and a book can be listed in up to 3 subcategories, not all coloring books will be listed under them. Thus for the sake of using a common denominator, we will use the sales rank within in the "Books" category for the purposes of discussing BSR.

By viewing the BSR you can get an approximate idea of the success of a book. The lower the number, the better. A BSR of 1 means your book is the top selling book on Amazon. A #1 book on Amazon will sell more than 2,000 copies every day. A BSR of 1,000,000 means there are 999,999 books selling better. 1,000,000 BSR will sell about 1 book every two to four weeks.

While adult coloring books are filling the best sellers lists, there are far more coloring books that are not selling at all. Think of it this way: If 18 out of the top 40 books are coloring books, how many coloring books are in the top 1,000,000, or 3,000,000, or 5,000,000?

For every one success, there are thousands that are lucky to see one or two sales per month.

Low sales can be a symptom of many things: artwork that doesn't appeal to the public, lack of marketing, too many competitors for the topic, or even just low seasonal demand.

Why CreateSpace?

In 2005, Amazon bought a company called CustomFlix, and renamed it to CreateSpace. Its original purpose was to print on-demand DVDs. Amazon expanded that to print on-demand books.

While CreateSpace is not the only print on demand service, it is integrated into Amazon.com and has one of the lowest printing costs on the market. For example: according to the CreateSpace Royalty Calculator, printing an 80 page, 8.5" x 11" black and white book with a list price of $14.95 will give you $6.80 royalty per book sold. Lulu.com will give you only $1.50 for the same selling price. CreateSpace's printing cost is lower, as well as their distribution costs. On the other hand, if you don't plan to sell on Amazon, Lulu's fees aren't nearly as bad since you aren't paying Amazon distribution fees.

Other POD services may have higher costs and tack on monthly fees, fees for making modifications, and more. If you use a local printer you have to buy copies of your book, which can mean significant out of pocket expenses and storage concerns.

CreateSpace handles selling your book on Amazon, including payment processing, customer service, delivery, and returns - and their royalties are excellent. This allows us to create a book, list it, and sit back while the money rolls in. We hope.

Equipment Requirements

To build a book for publishing on CreateSpace, you will need:

1. A desktop (or laptop) computer.

2. If you are drawing on paper, you'll need artist quality pen and paper, and flatbed scanner to import it into your computer. If you are making digital art then of course you will need the graphics/drawing programs of your choice.

3. Whether hand drawn or digitally created you will need to modify your art for publication using graphics software. There are a lot of commercial software tools available, but there are free alternatives that can work just as well.

That's it! The barrier to entry is quite low.

SELECTING A TOPIC FOR YOUR BOOK

Passion vs Business

If you're an artist you've probably been told to follow your passion and draw what you love regardless of whether or not it will make money. If drawing is your hobby, and you want to share it with the world via coloring books, that's fine. But you may not make money.

"Where the needs of the world and your talents cross, therein lies your vocation" --- Aristotle.

Making what you like ranks very low on the list of things that are important to become a commercial success. It might sound obvious, but if you want to make money, then you need to create something people want to buy.

I recently had a conversation with an artist who asked for my help. Her coloring book of freehand designs had made only one sale in the last four months. She had two one star reviews that said, "It looks like a child's scribbles!" and "Not worth the money." The second review posted pictures of the pages inside the book – something that generally helps sales, but in this case was the nail in the coffin. When I asked her what research she did before making the book, she admitted she didn't do any research at all.

"That's what I LIKE to draw!" She had a lot of fun making the pictures and was crushed when no one wanted to buy her book and have as much fun as she did coloring them in.

No matter how talented you are, if you do not use your talent to create FOR your audience, you will not sell coloring books.

Treating coloring books as a business doesn't mean you're selling out. Create something unique that stands out from the crowd and people will notice. If people want what they see, then you will be a success.

Therefore, selection of a topic or theme for your coloring book is both a personal and business decision. Your choice of topic should be one that showcases your unique talent and style, while also meeting your customers needs.

Market Research

What are your customers needs? Do you know? Do they know?

A common approach is to look at the market best sellers and then make something similar. You let someone else do the research and you piggyback. This approach may work, but its success is usually limited; if someone likes what is already out there, they will buy the existing best seller.

You may pick up sales from Amazon's "people also purchased" offerings.

Right now there are dozens of "Sweary" coloring books in the best seller's lists. Most of them are hastily thrown together by artists hoping to get in on a fad. But there are dozens more of the same theme that just aren't selling as well. The key to success when following fads is early entry, and aggressive marketing.

Alternatively, you can expand the existing market by putting your own personal twist or interpretation on the theme. There are dozens of high ranking coloring books featuring mandalas, geometrics, kaleidoscope designs, doodles, zentangles, books with real and fantasy animals, inspirational or obscene calligraphy and designs. Look through Amazon's listings for the theme and note down the BSR of each. Don't look through just the top 10. That's skimming the cream. Look at #100 in that theme. Look at #300. Which comes closest to your style? Will you be happy to do as well?

If you think you've found an unfilled need, or you can create a new niche market that doesn't yet exist, consider how you will market your book. It is one thing to create a coloring book that is unique. It is quite another to market it, especially on Amazon where searches are based on keywords that might not apply to your new book.

Keywords are words or phrases used in searches to find products the consumer wants to view.

Google Trends is a great tool that allows you to compare the popularity of keywords. You can compare "children coloring book" vs "adult coloring book". As you can see, the "children coloring book" search has flatlined, while "adult coloring book" is skyrocketing.

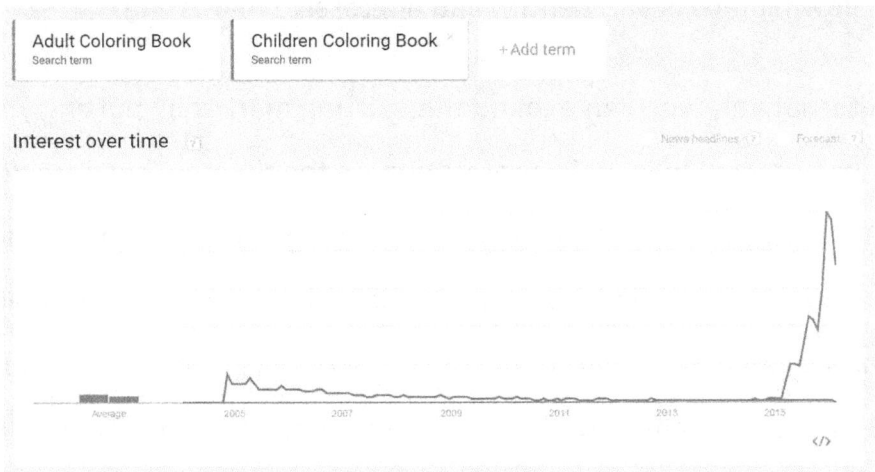

https://www.google.com/trends/

Even single terms are useful as they can show you trends and how often consumers look up those words. Search Google and Amazon to see if someone has already created the book you're planning. Since coloring books are popular it is not unusual to find not just one, but many variations on a theme. You need to determine if the topic is so crowded it will be hard to stand out or get people to take notice, or if the lack of availability is an indication there's a lack of demand. Are the existing books selling well? Is there room for you to join in? Can you do it better? If you can, then perhaps you can come to dominate the topic. If not, where do you think you'll sit among the competition? Being one of 3 gives you good odds, being one of 100 has little room for success. You don't want to get lost in a sea of new coloring books and slide down into oblivion. Depending on the answers to these questions, you might want to run with your original idea or look for a different topic.

Seasonal Books

Valentine's Day, Easter, Halloween, and Christmas bring many new seasonal themed coloring books. Seasonal books have very short lifespans. They can sell well, but they will only sell well for a short time. Next year and every year thereafter there will be more competition from newer books to take advantage of current fads. You should balance the time and effort you put into making a seasonal book against a general purpose book that sells year round.

I like to think about seasonal coloring books like going "all in" on a poker game. You'll either be one of the few who banks off the holiday, or your book will be sidelined most of the year. Big risk with big rewards.

Prohibited Content

CreateSpace has limits on what you can publish. Here are their content guidelines:

https://www.createspace.com/Help/Rights/ContentGuidelines.jsp

Most of the rules are vague; they basically tell you to follow your local laws, and that they reserve the right to deny for any reason they want. I find the final paragraph regarding public domain content interesting:

> *"Some types of content, such as public domain content, may be free to use by anyone, or may be licensed for use by more than one party. We will not accept content that is freely available on the web unless you are the copyright owner of that content. For example, if you received your content from a source that allows you and others to re-distribute it, and the content is freely available on the web, we will not accept it for sale through CreateSpace. We do accept public domain content, however we may request that you provide proof that your submitted material is actually in the public domain and may choose to not sell a public domain title if its content is undifferentiated or barely differentiated from one or more books already available through our service or available through other retail sites."*

While it doesn't appear that CreateSpace actively enforces this rule (it would be painful for them to research every book published), if they become aware you aren't following the guidelines, or if your book is reported, they will deactivate your book AND withhold royalties. Do not take Amazon's rules lightly.

MAKING YOUR ILLUSTRATIONS

Do you need artistic talent?

This is a tough question to answer.

You do not need talent to create original art, but stylish, attractive pictures will certainly inspire more people to purchase your book.

You can create your own art. You can hire an artist under a contract where you have copyright. You can purchase art with full rights. You can use art in the public domain so long as CreateSpace doesn't already have a similar book. Unfortunately, CreateSpace tends to approve everything and then, when there is a complaint, they will freeze your account and keep the royalties. You need to make sure you own the copyright or can prove public domain for the art you use BEFORE you publish your book, or you risk losing the royalties that book earns.

Many more people can use software to make mandalas, or hand-draw zentangles and doodles, than can draw realistic fairies and forest creatures. I realize some of these designs take a great deal of time and talent, but that is lost on a consumer who has two books side by side, one created in a few minutes by a web based program, and one painstakingly designed and hand drawn over the course of several days. All they care about is if the pictures look nice – are they attractive? So there will be more mandala, zentangle and doodle books on the market competing for the colorist's dollar.

Unless you have something truly extraordinary and/or market your book with vigor, if you are in a crowded theme you will likely see mediocre sales.

When it comes to analyzing the marketability of your art, you need to be your own harshest critic. You are going to spend days, weeks and for some people months, creating a coloring book. Unless you are doing it just so you can cross "publishing a book" off your bucket list, you're going to want people to buy the book you made.

Does your art have style? Is that style attractive to colorists? Have you actually colored-in your own pictures to be sure colorists of all levels can produce a pleasing finished product? Is the style consistent throughout a body of work e.g; can you make a group of pictures with similar theme and look? Is it in an over-saturated field or will it stand out from the crowd?

Digital vs Hand Drawn

I often see debates over whether digital art is "better" than hand drawn. It really doesn't matter if you have a stylus or a pen in your hand when you draw a picture, in the end all art must be digitized for publication. The results of both methods rely on the skill of the artist, and there are pros and cons to each. Use whatever gives you the results you want.

"Hand drawn" is a desirable keyword. Use that word in your title or description and your book will come up in search results by colorists who like the personalized, imperfect, and unique nature of hand drawn art.

Digital art gives you the opportunity to create original art in vectors, which will produce illustrations that are sharper, cleaner and more precise than hand drawn lines. Filters and manipulation programs (for mandalas and kaleidoscopic effects) make fast work of techniques that take many hours when hand drawn.

You can certainly use a combination of hand drawn and digital art, which I did when I wanted perfect circles for ornaments behind a hand drawn cat. You can also take your hand drawn art and convert it into vector, which will give you smooth and clean lines.

Hand Drawn

Hand drawn art is made with pen on paper. While techniques vary from artist to artist, many use a traditional process – make a rough graphite sketch on tracing or thin paper, refine the sketch, use a lightbox or transfer the graphite sketch to drawing paper, and make your final illustration. I like Bristol plate, but many people use vellum which also provides a crisp line. You can make your art any size, however there are a few things to consider:

1. If you draw larger than the intended print size and reduce down, your lines will look cleaner and sharper, while the reverse is true – if you enlarge a small picture the quality suffers.

2. Make sure your art will fit your scanner. Very large pieces of art will require multiple scans and stitching the picture together digitally, or specialized equipment which will incur more time and outside costs.

3. Your drawing surface should proportionally mirror the print area of your final book. To give a simple example: If your drawing fills an 8" x 10" piece of paper and your book is going to be printed 8" x 8", you'll need to crop off 2" from the height of your artwork.

Pen recommendations:

Rapidographs

Pigma Microns

Copic

Pitt

Paper recommendations:

Plate or Smooth Bristol

Vellum

Tracing paper

Digital Artwork

Digital artwork is done on a computer. Either by drawing lines directly in software using a mouse, or emulating pen and paper using a tablet/digitizer interface. If you create art digitally you don't need to scan your illustration and there is no post-cleanup to do. On the other hand, drawing on the computer, even with a tablet, requires a different skill set than traditional hand drawn art and may be difficult to master for those used to drawing with pen and paper. I find it hard to work at the same speed with a mouse or tablet, and the quality of my art suffers. Yet, many people find it more comfortable and faster working with a stylus and graphics program. Choose what works best for you.

One of the major issues I have with drawing on my Wacom tablet is drawing lines that are jittery. There are several software options that can help smooth out your lines – my favorite is a plugin called Lazy Nezumi. It has a dozen or so different options to smooth lines, and it has a free trial so you can try it before you buy it.

Product Recommendations:

Inkscape (free)   https://inkscape.org

GIMP (free)   https://www.gimp.org/

Photoshop   http://www.adobe.com/products/photoshop.html

Illustrator   http://www.adobe.com/products/illustrator.html

Grayscale

Grayscale pictures are exactly as the name suggests – they are pictures that only contain shades of gray. They can be hand drawn graphite, charcoal, ink illustrations, digital drawings, but they are most commonly paintings or photographs that have been saved in grayscale mode in a graphics program. Artistic and brushstroke filters can be used to add texture.

Pictures on your computer or the internet are already in digital format. Artwork and photographs must be scanned to a digital format, opened in a photographic manipulation program, and filters applied to achieve the desired results.

For the purpose of a commercial coloring book that you want to publish via CreateSpace, be sure to use only original pictures where you are the copyright holder.

You may not use photographs or art if you do not own the copyright.

Do not use random pictures you find online. Do not directly trace or cut and paste parts of a picture. Do not modify existing pictures. Someone made that art, someone took that picture – and it was not you. If you purchase a license to use art you did not create yourself, be sure it is the appropriate license and you can produce it when questioned.

Size Matters

Before you make your illustrations you will need to determine what size you want your book to be. The size of your book will determine the dimensions of your artwork. CreateSpace can print books as small as 5" x 8" to as large as 8.5" x 11". You can bleed your images – which means to run them off the page – by making the art .25 of an inch larger than the page size. The additional area is cropped off but allows for a margin of error in the cutting process.

Many colorists prefer the art to be constrained within margins. CreateSpace requires at least a 0.25" border that must be kept clear of text and graphics. Additionally, the side of the page that touches the binding needs an even larger margin. This inside margin will vary based on how many pages your book contains, as thicker books require slightly more white space to account for the book not laying as flat.

Margin specifications:

Page Count	Inside Margin	Outside Margins
24 to 150 pages	0.375"	At least 0.25"
151 to 300 pages	0.500"	At least 0.25"
301 to 500 pages	0.625"	At least 0.25"
501 to 700 pages	0.750"	At least 0.25"
701 to 828 pages	0.875"	At least 0.25"

If you use the exact margins CreateSpace recommends, their measurements may not match up with the software you are using, and that may result with your book being rejected when you submit for approval. It's best to leave a bit more margin than the minimum.

Warning: CreateSpace may cut a book to a different size than expected. Each printed book may have small variations in size as different machines cut the paper. It's not uncommon to see a book cut shorter by 0.25" – 0.35". I recommend a 0.5" outside margin to account for the variation in book size. It also looks good and colorists don't have to color right to the edge of the paper.

The CreateSpace recommendation for the inside margin is based on text books, not coloring books. Content closest to the binding of the book will not lay as flat as the outside and thus become harder to access for coloring. When using 0.5" for the outside margins, I like using a 1" inside margin.

When using 0.5" margin for the outside and 1" for the inside, your illustration size will be 7" x 10":

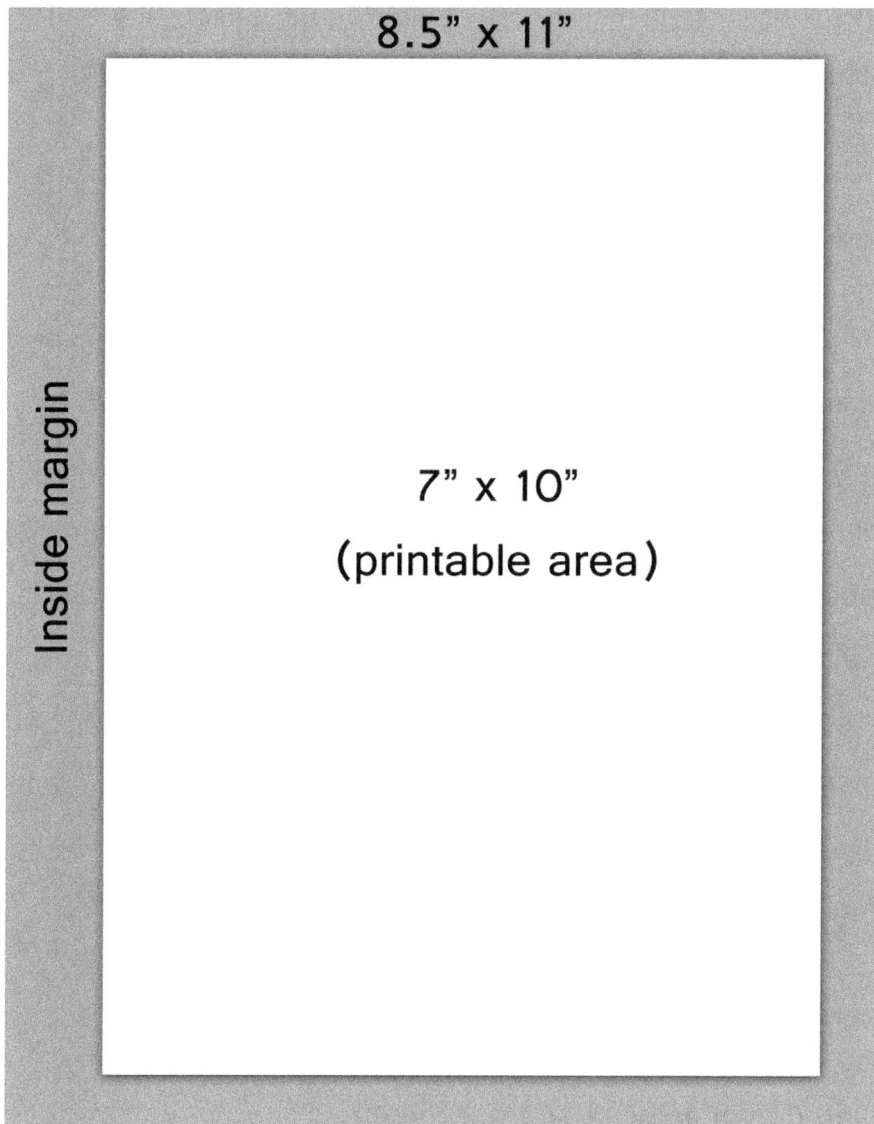

8.5" x 11"

Inside margin

7" x 10"
(printable area)

You don't have to draw your artwork in a 7" x 10" area, but it will have to conform to those proportions or you will be forced to crop out some of your image to make it fit.

An alternative to cropping is to distort the image by stretching or squeezing it in a graphics manipulation program. I prefer cropping because elements within the picture can be distorted by non-proportional manipulation.

How many illustrations?

How many illustrations should you make for a book? Based on my research, most coloring books contain anywhere from 20 to 100 illustrations. When colorists are surveyed, the majority look for a large number of illustrations in books printed on medium grade paper featuring mandalas, zentangles, doodles and such, but as few as 15 - 20 illustrations if they are highly artistic. Your best bet is to look at how many illustrations are included in coloring books closest to your own, and follow suit. Too few pictures and people may consider other books. Too many and you might have been able to release two books instead of one.

Scanning Pictures

Hand drawn artwork and non-digitized photographs require a flatbed scanner to import into your computer. You will need a photo manipulation program such as Photoshop or Gimp as well as a scanner large enough to hold your photographs and art flat on the scanning bed.

There are many software settings with a scanner, but in general you want to scan line art as either grayscale or color, and with the highest resolution allowed. If you are in the market for a new scanner, look for one that can scan at least 600 DPI.

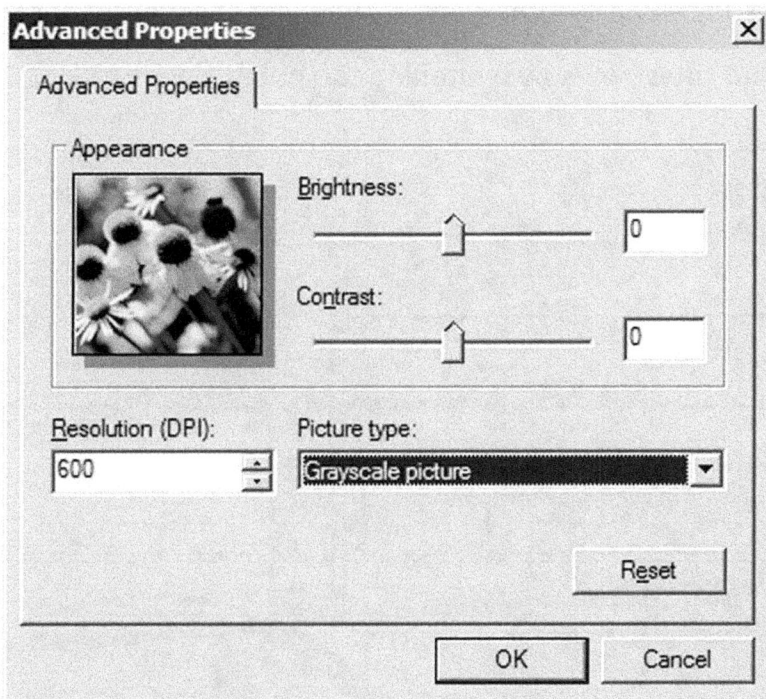

Once the illustration has been scanned, you'll need to clean up your hand drawn image. You will almost always see stray dust, hairs, etc, that get picked up by the scanner, and of course there are almost always a few smudges and overdrawn or weak lines to repair.

It is better to repair these things digitally than to white them out with paint on the original. If you use paint you may find yourself touching up those areas to remove shadows from see-through and brush strokes.

Due to variations in scanners, paper, and line quality, you should verify your black lines are really black and your whites are really white. Failure to do so will result in halftones being printed in the book, something you will want to avoid. Just be careful not to blow out your finest lines by whitening too much.

You can adjust using brightness and contrast tools, but I find that the "Levels" tool in Photoshop does a better job. Pull the slider on the left to darken dark, and the slider on the right to lighten whites:

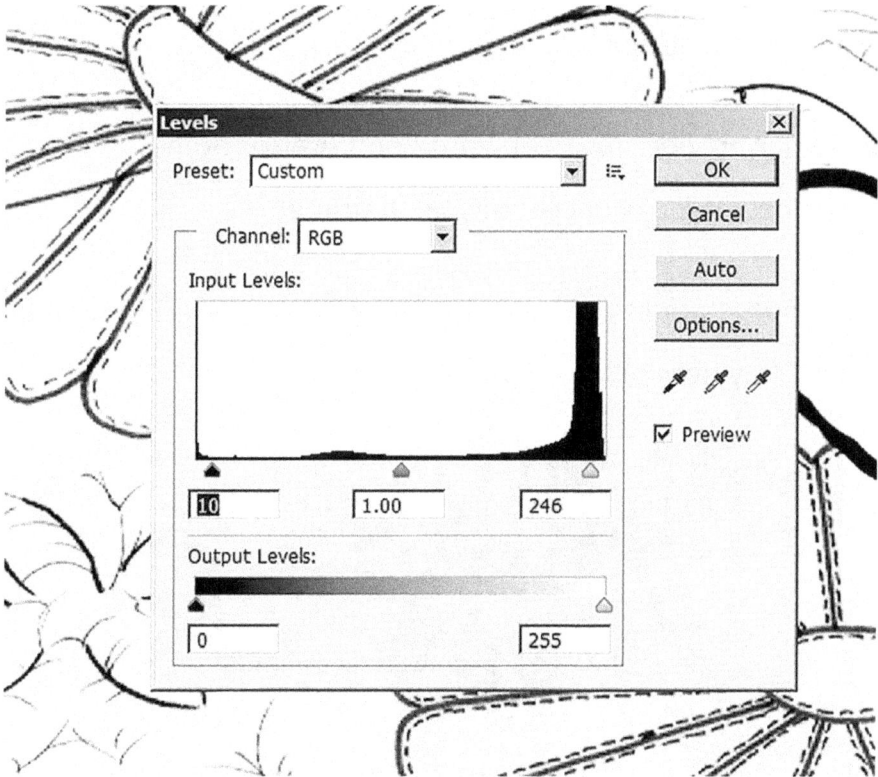

Once you've made adjustments, you can confirm that your whites are white and blacks are black by using the Color Picker tool. Simply select the dark lines to see if they are pure black (#000000) and white areas are #ffffff. If they aren't, keep adjusting brightness/ contrast/levels as needed.

Be sure to convert the image to black and white or grayscale if you haven't already. Ideally your images will be K-only (black) to limit confusion at the printer, but grayscale works well too. You will find greater consistency by limiting the number of conversions CreateSpace has to perform.

Line Considerations

How your artwork looks on your computer or home printer may not be how it looks once it has been printed.

CreateSpace prints at 444 ppi on 60# white paper. They do this by making tiny dots of ink on paper:

Lines can look solid black to the eye but will appear in the printed book as halftones, where the dots will be spaced further apart to emulate gradients. Lines that are close together may also fill in with halftone.

Halftones are not inherently bad, and in fact some colorists prefer their art shaded by halftones. But that is a small market, and in general such anomalies of the print process tend to make your book look less professional and "cheap". Even a disposable $50 inkjet printer will not produce visible halftones!

The best way to avoid most halftones is by limiting the size of the pens you use in your illustration, and making sure those pens are fresh. This eliminates the temptation to pick up a very fine pen or danger of using a pen that is low on ink which may lack blackness and skip.

Greatly enlarged hand drawn art using .005 and .01 Pigma Micron pens, printed through CreateSpace:

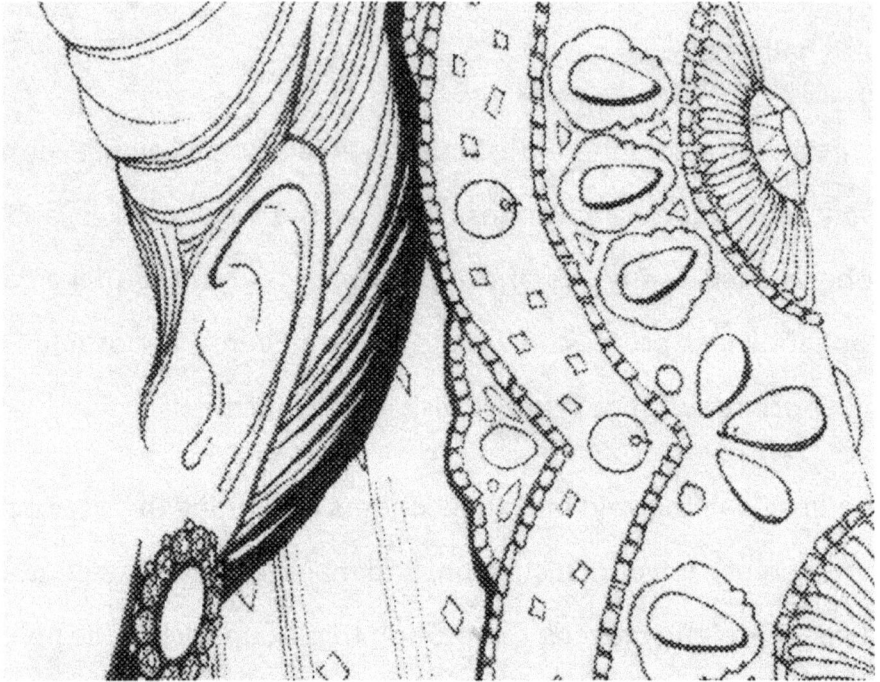

You can see white dots within the large black line, and the vertical lines under the ear appear as lines of dots rather than the fine solid lines I actually drew. You can use an image manipulation tool of choice and boost the levels till the lines are pure black, but this leaves artifacts, closes in the white areas, will gray up the background color and create a muddy look. Go too far the other way and finer lines begin to break up until they completely disappear.

How to Avoid Halftones

Hand drawn art will always have some halftones. Your original art will vary in thickness and depth of color and the process of digitizing will call for compromise.

Results will vary depending on your level of skill.

With digital vector artwork, you don't have to worry about half-tones. Proper settings will ensure all of your lines will be 100% black and the background 100% white.

Of course you can import your hand drawn art into a graphics program and trace the lines as vectors on a new layer. This isn't recommended for finished art as it's duplicating your efforts and all your artwork will now take twice as long to create.

However, it works quite well if you import your sketch to a graphics program and make your finished art digitally.

For most artists, just cleaning up their hand drawn image and al-lowing some halftones is acceptable. Depending on your illustration it may not matter or even be noticeable. This option allows your artwork to retain its hand drawn character.

Raster vs Vector

When you scan your artwork, or when you are painting digitally, your image will be raster. Meaning, the illustration is made up of tiny little dots, each one containing a color and position. Combined, they create your image.

Example of a raster image (zoomed in to show details):

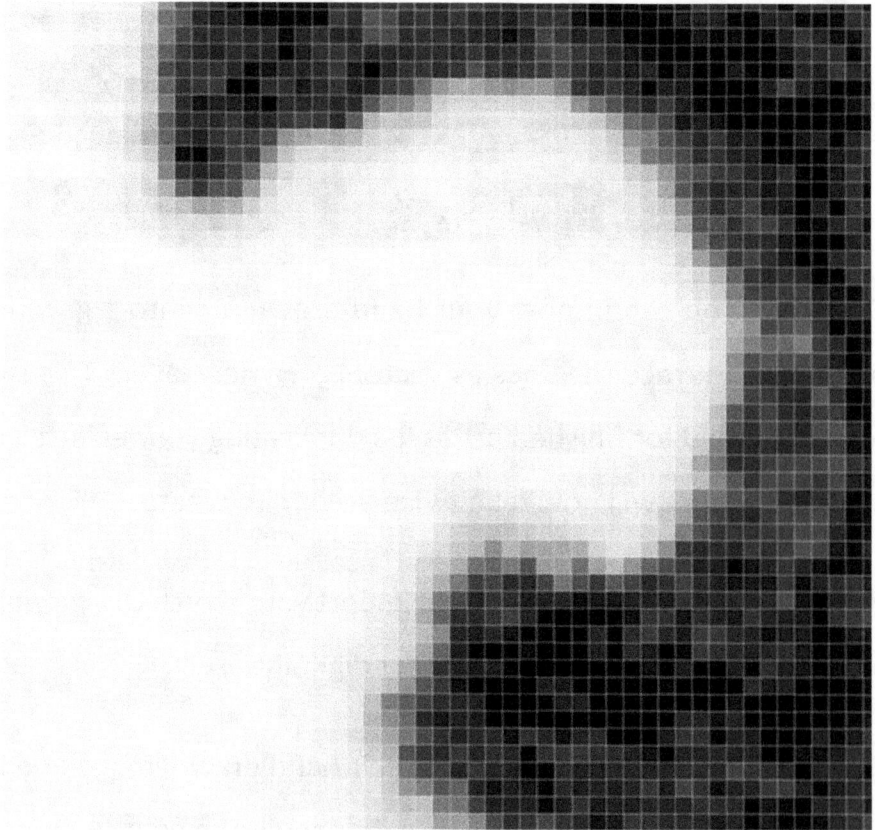

Even if you are diligent with all hand drawn lines in your artwork, and they are all solid with pure black, there are inherent issues with pen and paper: Take pen to paper and then scan and enlarge. You'll see it's darkest in the center of the line. The outside edges of the line will have less ink soaked into the paper than the center, causing the line to fade away at the edges, like the image on the left. When printed through CS, this will give you little dots, or halftones, around the edges of your lines.

One way around that choppy halftone edge is vector images.

Vector images use geometrical primitives (prims) instead of tiny dots when describing the image. Rather than describing each of the 20,000 points in a rectangle, vector will describe the rectangle as: "line color = black x1 = 1, y1 = 1 x2 = 2000, y2 = 1000". It is a lot less effort to describe, and can make the image size much smaller. Vector has the added bonus of making your illustration resolution independent. This means we can scale the image larger and smaller without any loss of quality. Instead of zooming in on the tiny dots of raster images, vectors scale by increasing the size of the lines drawn mathematically. Example: to enlarge our black rectangle, we'd change "x2 = 2000 y2 = 1000" from the above example, to "x2 = 4000 y2 = 2000".

Even with vector images, you will still see halftones in the finished publication if your lines aren't pure black (#000000). If you use blue or gray to visually enhance your image, those colors are not pure black and will be screened by the print process.

Converting Raster Images to Vector

Hand drawn art saved as a raster image can be converted to vector. Adobe Illustrator is commonly used to do this, but there are free options, such as Inkscape's "Trace Bitmap".

I'll use Adobe Illustrator (known as AI) in this example to show how easy it is:

Import your scanned artwork into AI, and click on Window > Image Trace. Click on the image, and then the image trace window options will become active.

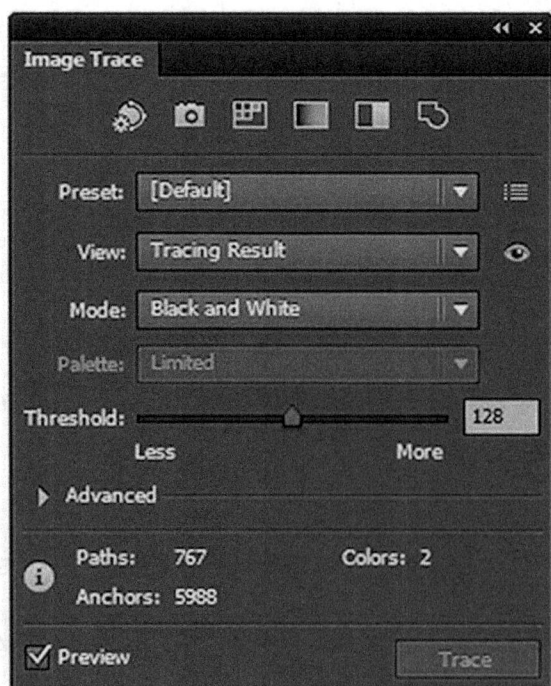

With the Preview option enabled, you can adjust the settings to see what works best for your artwork. Tweak how many points are used, number of colors, preview the smoothness of your lines at various points, and so on.

Below is a close up view of a page printed in CreateSpace. The illustration was originally a hand drawn cat, later converted to vector. All areas that are solid black have smooth lines. If you look closely around the eyes, bridge of the nose, and whiskers, you will notice lines not 100% black still contains halftones despite this being a vector image, but it has been cleaned up to a very acceptable level.

To illustrate the differences more clearly, here is the same cat's eye printed on CreateSpace. The left eye is from a 1,200 DPI scan, printed as raster.

On the right is the same artwork, but converted to vector in Adobe Illustrator. You can see the vector presets made some of the lines gray, which resulted in halftones, but the thing I want to point out, is that the lines in the vector image are completely solid, with no halftones at the edges. This makes them smooth and visibly sharper to the naked eye.

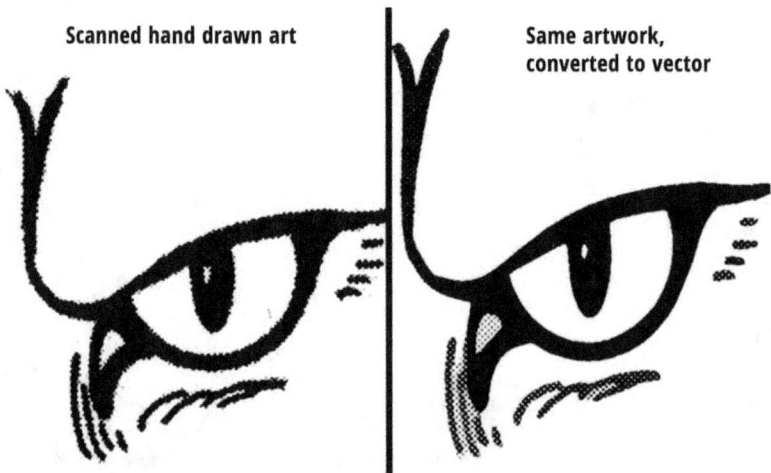

Scanned hand drawn art — Same artwork, converted to vector

Regardless, if your artwork is sent to CreateSpace as raster or vector, all artwork must be converted to raster for printing.

Thus, if I took the hand drawn cat's eye, converted it to vector, then made it a raster image again, it would print closer to the vector example on the right, than the raster on the left.

Long story short: Vector isn't needed for great lines. The process of converting artwork to vector eliminates the edges of your lines that aren't perfectly black, which results in sharper prints.

ASSEMBLING THE COVER

Colorists DO judge books by their covers. In fact, your cover is the most important page in your entire CreateSpace book, as Amazon defaults to only show the cover of the book on the product page, and the front cover in its various categories and search results. Your cover needs to represent the book's content while capturing the attention of the consumer as they browse Amazon. This means you need to consider how the cover looks full sized when printed, as well as how it looks when shrunk down to thumbnail sized (160x160 pixels):

Cats & Quilts: Adult Coloring Book Sep 23, 2015
by Jason Hamilton
Paperback
$8.31 $9.99 Prime   ☆☆☆☆☆ ▾ 69
Get it by Monday, Feb 15
More Buying Choices
$7.21 used & new (35 offers)

Color Me Beautiful, Women of the World: Adult Coloring Book Jan 15, 2016
by Jason Hamilton
Paperback
$8.99 $9.99 Prime   ☆☆☆☆☆ ▾ 21
Get it by Monday, Feb 15
More Buying Choices
$8.87 used & new (20 offers)

Santa's Cats: Christmas Adult Coloring Book Oct 31, 2015
by Jason Hamilton
Paperback
$9.99 Prime   ☆☆☆☆☆ ▾ 20
Get it by Monday, Feb 15
More Buying Choices
$7.21 used & new (28 offers)

Regardless if your interior is black and white or full color, your cover will be printed in full color. Take advantage of this in order to catch the eye of shoppers! They will be browsing through hundreds of other books, you want something they will see, take notice, and click to buy.

The print quality of the cover is excellent. You will not visibly see any halftones and the colors are vibrant. Here is an example from one of my book's covers:

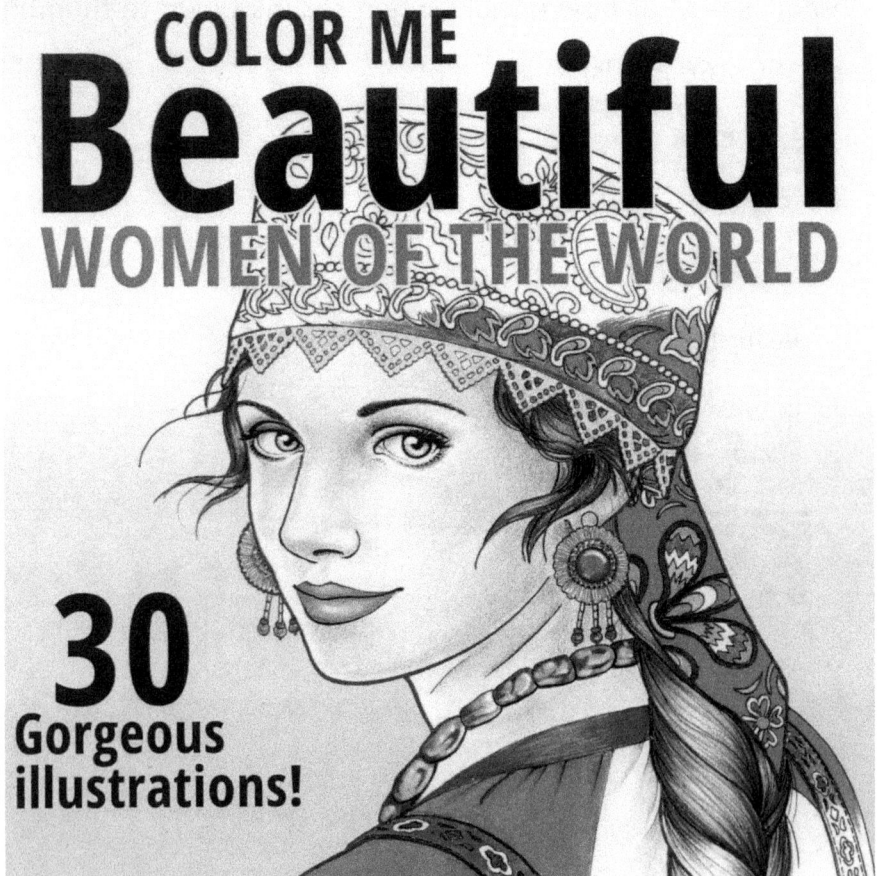

COLOR ME **Beautiful**
WOMEN OF THE WORLD

30
Gorgeous
illustrations!

CreateSpace has made building a cover easy, offering online cover builders and professional services.

But, since your illustrations are a unique representation of your talent, and CreateSpace offers templates to make building your cover easy, why not design the cover yourself?

CreateSpace basic cover templates:

https://www.createspace.com/Help/Book/Artwork.do

Just enter your book specifications and how many pages, and you'll be able to download a pdf and png properly sized for your cover. I design my covers using Photoshop, but the free alternative, Gimp, will work fine too.

Overlay your own design on the downloaded cover template, and export as a PDF for publishing. Page count matters because it determines the width of the spine. Be sure the number of pages in the book and the template match exactly. Oddly enough, CreateSpace lacks a 8.5" x 11" template. Bookow has a template generator that not only has 8.5" x 11", but it generates templates with your ISBN number built into the bar code:

http://bookow.com/resources.php

Page Layout Size = Full Bleed Size
The full cover size including bleed
17.430" X 11.250"
(442.72mm X 285.75mm)

Black Dotted Line = Trim Edge
The trim size of this cover including spine
17.180" X 11.000"
(436.38mm X 279.44mm)

White Area = Live Area
Position logos, text, and essential images in this area.

Red Area = Out of Live/Bleed
Your background artwork must fill the red area.
Do not place logos, text,
or essential images in the red area.
If your artwork does not meet these
requirements, it may be rejected.

Visit www.bookow.com for more free tools for self-publishers,
including a barcode generator, and a formula hyphenizer.
We provide POD and e-book layout and formatting services.

Back
8.5" X 11"
(215.9mm X 279.4mm)

CreateSpace
**Paperback Book
Cover Template**
Prepared by www.bookow.com

8.5" X 11" Book
(215.9mm X 279.4mm)

80 pages

0.180" Spine Width
(4.58mm)

White Paper

Turn off
guidelines
for final art
Whatever is visible
will be printed

Front
8.5" X 11"
(215.9mm X 279.4mm)

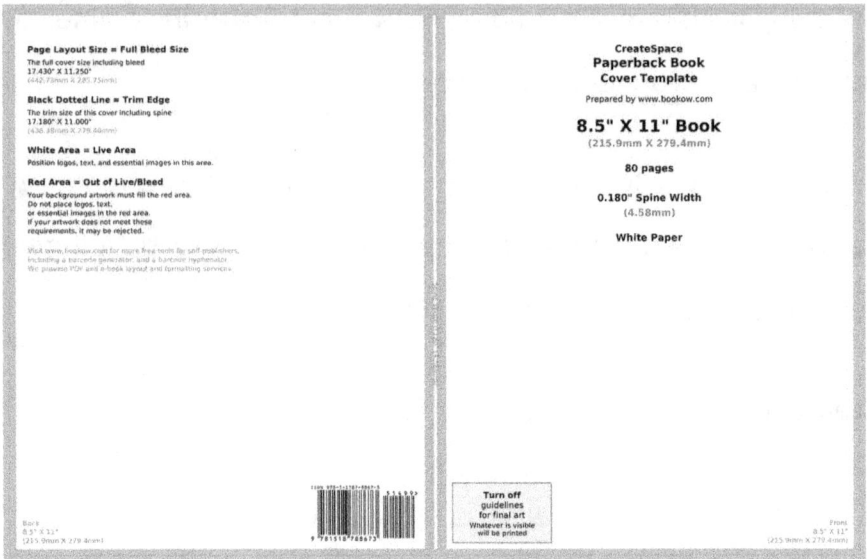

WARNING! CreateSpace is not accurate in placement of covers or cutting books to the proper size. This means a cover might see a shift of 0.25" or more. I've also seen my cover rotated approximately 3 degrees.

Be careful not to place anything important near the bleed margins or they could be cut off. I've had my 8.5" x 11" books get printed at 8.3" x 10.7"! This also means any text on the spine can be shifted by 0.25" as well, so unless your book is 200+ pages long, adding text to the spine is going to be extremely risky and may result with the spine text partially appearing on the front or rear cover.

Here is an example of my book being cut too short. It sits on top of a properly sized 8.5" x 11" book:

Barcode Color

You don't need to settle for just white background with your bar-code. Bowker's website says:

"Reds, yellows, and white are suitable background colors if there are no black, blue or green constituents. Blues and greens, provided they are not too pale, and black are good colors for the image."

Glossy or Matte?

Originally, CreateSpace only printed covers with a glossy finish. In early 2014, they started printing with matte as well. There is no cost difference between the two. CreateSpace claims matte is more durable, but I don't find glossy to be fragile.

I've found that the matte finish shows off greasy fingerprints just as easily as the glossy finish.

CreateSpace allows for a maximum cover PDF file size of 40 MB.

I typically flatten my cover, export with no compression, then check to see if it is below 40 MB. If it isn't, I export again with maximum compression specified in the PDF export. If the file size still isn't below 40 MB, I'll try with high compression instead. The goal is to use the least amount of compression possible.

ASSEMBLING THE INTERIOR

General Notes

Make sure your images are 300 DPI or greater. While the printing process currently doesn't print with finer detail with 600 or 1,200 DPI images, using higher resolution images will not hurt. If CreateSpace ever replaces existing printing hardware with one that can print with higher resolution, by using 600 or 1,200 DPI images, your future books may automatically take advantage of this. High resolution scans of your artwork will also allow you to expand your lineup to include sales of poster prints, t-shirts and more. The only drawback to higher resolution images is increased disk size and higher CPU and memory requirements when editing them. I cannot tell the difference between my images at 300 vs 600 DPI when printed in CreateSpace.

Use a lossless format when possible. JPEG is lossy, meaning that when the image is saved, it compresses the image with an approximation of where pixels are located. This degrades the image, and can introduce visible artifacts.

For raster images, my recommendation is compressed png, which despite the name, is lossless.

For vector images, use EPS when possible. EPS stands for Encapsulated PostScript. It is a self contained file format that is designed specifically for vector images.

After running dozens of print tests with CreateSpace using various different image file formats and resolutions, I found the very best print results have always come from a vector within an EPS.

Second best will come from raster (generated from a vector). To the naked eye, they will look almost identical. But zooming in reveals that the lines are not quite as sharp.

The slight differences between these two methods are so slight that you'd be hard pressed to pick which print had better lines without the use of a magnifying glass.

On page 127 is a chapter titled **REFRENCE ILLUSTRATIONS** that has an illustrated printed in a variety of different resolutions and file formats so that you can judge for yourself.

Templates

CreateSpace has premade interior templates available online:

https://www.createspace.com/Products/Book/InteriorPDF.jsp

Find a template that matches your book size, open it in Word or

OpenOffice, then drag and drop your illustrations into the template.

If you've chosen to print one sided, make sure your illustrations and odd number pages are on the LEFT side of each spread. That will result in a finished product with the illustrations on the RIGHT hand page.

The major drawback with using a text editor to publish is that the formatting tools are extremely basic and any lines added on a page will push all subsequent pages down by that same amount. This will force you to reformat the entire document multiple times as you add and modify content.

MS Publisher or Adobe InDesign are better publishing platforms. But for your first book, you can publish using OpenOffice without having to learn a new tool or paying for additional software.

Interior Content

At a minimum your book should contain a title page, a copyright page, and your illustrations.

Title

This page will list your book's title and your author name. It's nice to include a graphic (such as a company logo) to fill up the page.

Copyright

List whatever copyright disclaimer you want. I like to say "Copyright 2016, Jason Hamilton, all rights reserved". I also inform the user that they have permission to post copies of my artwork online as part of a book review. Reviews and examples of artwork are important for gaining sales on Amazon, so I like to make sure they know its OK to share. I also use this page to provide contact information so that consumers can get in touch with me, listing my email address and website URL.

Illustrations

It goes without saying that you should include your artwork in your coloring book. Colorists favor one sided pages.

There are also optional pages that you should consider adding:

Colored by

Very popular these days is a page after the copyright that has a graphic the colorist can color, and a section to write their name and date to memorialize the book as belonging to them and something they have colored-in.

Buy My Other Books

If you've published more than one book, you should consider making the last page in your book an advertisement to inform the user that you have other titles available. For my ad, I show sample illustrations and display my website URL as a place to find my other books and free printables and tutorials. You can also ask for an honest review if the buyer likes the book.

Single Sided Pages

In survey after survey, colorists prefer single sided images. With CreateSpace, the cost to print a black and white book containing 80 pages is the same as printing 40 pages. There is no extra cost to the author to meet this basic requirement of our customers.

CreateSpace uses medium weight, 60 lb bond paper, which is fine for text based books and children's coloring books. However, it is just "acceptable" for adult coloring books. As the genre grows, so too do the requirements of our colorists who use advanced (and often expensive) products and treat each picture as a work of art.

CreateSpace paper has limitations. If you print an image on both sides you will see a shadow of each image on the other side of the paper. When pages are colored-in with pencils, the point will make indentations that carry through to the other side of the page, and wet media such as markers and gel pens may bleed through and ruin any image that has been printed there.

Single sided pages allow colorists to put something under the picture to prevent indentations and bleed through, some will remove the page (be sure to leave a good spine side margin so they can avoid the print area when removing the image) and color it outside of the book, some will copy the picture onto card stock or watercolor paper. But be warned, some will complain about the paper quality, as they want nothing less than spiral bound card stock – which CreateSpace does not provide and would make the book prohibitively expensive for most buyers.

Exporting the Interior

Once you've assembled your interior, you'll need to save it as a .doc or .pdf. While .doc will work, you give up a lot of advanced functionality and options. You also leave it up to CreateSpace as to how they will interpret your .doc file and margins may not be what you expect.

Thus .pdf is highly recommended:

PDF allows you to export your book exactly as you want it to look. PDF allows you to embed the fonts you used so that the printed document looks the way you expect.

Use the "PDF/X-1a" pdf standard when exporting.

Select the highest possible image quality, and don't down sample.

The maximum file size CreateSpace allows is 400 MB.

If your exported pdf is larger than that, change your image quality from maximum to a lower setting till the size fits.

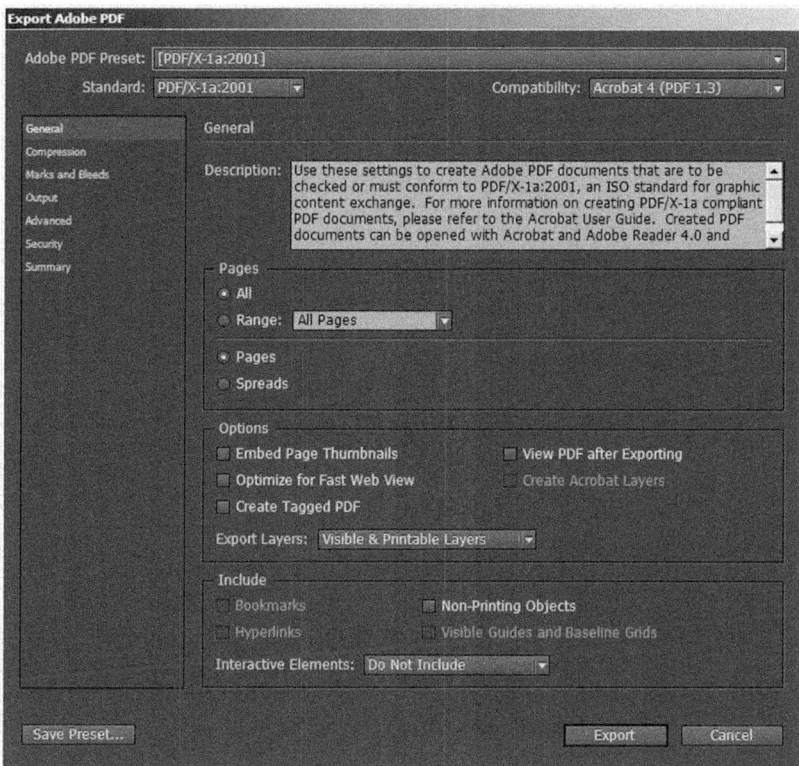

PUBLISHING ON CREATESPACE

CreateSpace will literally walk you through publishing your book step by step. You just need to fill in your details, name the book, and upload your cover and interior.

I won't bother going into the details of each step since they are mostly self explanatory – however there are a few steps that you should pay attention to:

Title and Description

The title of your book does more than describe the contents of the book. It is a tool to gain the attention of consumers.

Your title and description are going to be used by Amazon in order to match up user searches with products.

It is important to optimize keywords used in your title to focus on the kinds of searches you think will best sell your book, all while also accurately describing it. Search engines not only pair matching words, but they will match based on closeness of the words. For example, if someone searched for "red flower", it would match a book with the title "A red flower" better than it would match "Red tea flower". Word order and distance between the words will matter.

There are additional considerations Amazon takes into account, such as Sales Rank, which we'll get into in a later chapter.

Fortunately you don't have to guess at what keywords are popular. As mentioned earlier, Google Trends allows you to compare key-words to see how often they are searched for in Google. Look again at the result for "children coloring book". It has a deep downward spiral showing that users on Google are searching for it less and less. This helps me avoid those keywords when writing my book description and title.

When selecting keywords for your title, be careful not to over-optimize. Stacking too many keywords will make your title incoherent and no one will bother reading it. I see some books that have completely incoherent titles that appear to be nothing more than a collection of most searched for keywords, which makes me wonder if their authors have any command of the English language at all. Don't optimize for the search engine, optimize it for your customer. Like your cover, it should be catchy, easy to remember, and ideally contain words that users would likely search for to find your book.

Once your book is published, the title information will be locked and you will no longer be able to make changes.

CreateSpace's policy is not to adjust this information, but I've had success contacting CreateSpace on the phone and having them make minor adjustments to my subtitle. For any major changes, such as a new title, author name, or book dimensions, a new ISBN will be required.

ISBN

ISBN is an acronym for International Standard Book Number. It is a unique 10 or 13 digit number assigned to every published book. It allows a person to look up any book to find out who the publisher is, book title and author name, as well as things like binding type and page size.

The ISBN is typically printed inside the book on the copyright page, as well as on the lower right side of the rear cover, along with a scannable barcode.

CreateSpace offers 4 different ISBN options:

CreateSpace Assigned, Custom, Custom Universal, and Provide Your Own.

1. CreateSpace-Assigned ISBN

This option is completely free. The assigned ISBN can only be used on CreateSpace. Meaning that you can't have your book printed with your local printer and sell copies on eBay using this ISBN. If you are planning to sell your book exclusively through CreateSpace, this is an excellent choice to get your feet wet with no money out of pocket.

2. Custom ISBN

This option costs $10. It is almost exactly the same as the CreateSpace-Assigned ISBN, except that you can define the imprint name. Imprint name is a fancy word for publisher name. When your book is listed for sale on Amazon, under Product Details section, it will show: "Publisher: CreateSpace". With the custom ISBN option, you can change the publisher name to reflect your name or your company name. It has no other benefit beyond masking that you are publishing your book through CreateSpace.

Why do it? CreateSpace is widely known as a print on demand service. Masking the use of CreateSpace can make your book appear more professional. On the flip side, colorists who buy a lot of coloring books would know what kind of paper and print quality to expect from a CreateSpace title. This means if someone hates the paper thickness of CreateSpace, they'd know what to expect from your book. By masking that you use CreateSpace, you might end up with a poor review you might have otherwise been able to avoid.

My opinion is that the custom ISBN is not worth the money, as most consumers won't notice the subtle change in the product description. Furthermore, you can buy your own ISBN for less than $10! (see Provide Your Own ISBN)

3. Custom Universal ISBN

With the custom option, you are buying a single ISBN from Bowker (the company that manages the ISBN database) with CreateSpace acting as a middle man. You'll own this ISBN and can use it anywhere, including other POD services and your local printer. If this was a free option, it would have no drawbacks compared to any of the two previous choices - it gives you the ability to define your imprint name and allows you to have your book printed outside of CreateSpace with no additional changes. Unfortunately it costs $99, and as such it is not a good deal unless you plan to only ever publish a single book.

4. Provide Your Own ISBN

You can purchase ISBNs directly from Bowker using their sales site: https://www.myidentifiers.com

This option is just like the Custom Universal ISBN option except that you're cutting out the middle man and buying from the source.

Bowker will sell 10 ISBNs for $295 ($29.50 each), or 100 ISBNs for $575 ($5.75 each). While neither option is cheap, you get substantial savings over the single ISBN purchase by buying in bulk.

For anyone serious about making coloring books, 10 ISBNs can be exhausted within 1-2 years. If you plan on, or think it is possible that you will create more than 10 coloring books, then the only correct choice will be to buy the 100 block since buying two sets of 10 ISBNs will exceed the cost of the 100.

Bowker doesn't list prices beyond 100 on their website, but the cost for 1,000+ ISBNs is around $1 per ISBN.

I know what you're thinking - buy 1,000 ISBNs then sell individual ISBNs to friends for less than they can buy them! Sadly, the ISBN Terms Of Use specifically prohibits doing this:

"Registrant will only assign ISBNs to publications to which it holds publishing rights.

Registrant will not sell, license, distribute, disseminate, assign or otherwise make its assigned ISBN prefix and ISBNs available to other publishers or to any third parties.

Once a title has been published with an ISBN, it cannot be re-used or modified. However regardless of which ISBN option you choose, you can always publish a second edition of your book with a different ISBN, and in doing so, adjust title, author, etc."

Thus you should only buy what you think you will need for your lifetime.

Question: I'd like to migrate from a CreateSpace assigned ISBN to my own ISBN purchased through Bowker. Will I lose all my reviews?

Initially yes, but you can fix that. When you publish your book a second time under a new ISBN, CreateSpace will need to be notified so that Amazon won't sell the same title twice. CreateSpace will mark your original title as "retired". The new title will start out as any new book would – with zero reviews and no sales rank. You are starting over from scratch.

But it doesn't need to end there - once your new title is active and listed on Amazon, you can contact CreateSpace a second time and ask that the two titles be merged. The reviews between the two books will be merged, meaning that either product page on Amazon will show all reviews left for either book. The new listing will have a link that says "See all formats and editions". Clicking it will expand the section to show all editions of your book, including the retired edition. While CreateSpace will tell you that the merge process will take approximately 3 to 5 business days, I have seen my new title obtain the reviews from the original title within 20 minutes. Other features, such as the carousel at the top of the Author Central page may take weeks to update.

Question: Why does Library and Academic distribution require a CreateSpace ISBN?

CreateSpace has a partnership with Baker & Taylor to distribute books to libraries and schools. You can only make use of this channel with a CreateSpace ISBN. That said, libraries and schools do not exclusively purchase books through CreateSpace, and its exclusion will not likely impact your sales.

Color or black and white?

CreateSpace will print your interior in either color or black and white. If you select color, CS will consider all pages within your book color, and charge you accordingly, even if some are black and white.

Here are the technical specs between the two options:

Black and white:	60# white 444ppi
Full color:	60# white 426ppi

They are very close, but the main difference between the two is cost: Your royalties for an 8.5" x11" black and white book containing 80 pages with a list price of $11.99 is $5.04. If you opt for color, your royalty will be $0.74. To make the same $5 royalty per color book sold, you'd have to raise the list price of the color book 36% to just under $20! How many coloring books have you seen selling for

$20 that are printed on 60# paper? Not a lot, I suspect, as colorists expect much higher quality paper stock for that price.

BISAC category

This is a book category system that helps identify the type of content inside the book. In 2015, BISG (Book industry Study Group) added "Games / Activity Books (includes Coloring Books)", code GAM019000. Unfortunately Amazon has not yet updated CreateSpace, so we cannot select it. For the time being, I use "Nonfiction / Art / Drawing", "Art / General", or "Art / Mixed media", other artists might choose mental health or philosophical or theme related categories. No choice is going to be a 100% match. Amazon automatically assigns a matching Amazon category based on this selection. Examples, if you select "Art / Mixed Media" as your BISAC category, you'll automatically get "Books > Other Media > Mixed Media" on Amazon.

Amazon representatives may assign up to two additional Amazon categories, for a total of three. My books have always been assigned three, but when I speak with Amazon representatives on the phone, they tell me the policy is to assign two categories for CreateSpace books, the third is limited to publishing houses. This seems to vary widely depending on which person I speak with, so your mileage may vary.

List Price

Your book should be priced fairly for the consumer.

Compensating you, the author, for your time and effort really doesn't come into play.

Consider Jack and Jill. They each spend two weeks to make 30 pictures. They both made the same financial investment in materials and computer equipment necessary to produce a coloring book file to upload to CreateSpace. They each price their coloring book at $6.99.

Jack's sales are terrible and buyers are saying his book is overpriced. Meanwhile Jill's book is getting glowing reviews and her price is considered highly competitive. Why? Because buyers LIKE Jill's book more than they like Jack's book. The amount of time and effort you put into a book is irrelevant. An experienced graphic designer could set up the interior of a coloring book in an hour, while my first book took several days and several rejections by CreateSpace until I got it right.

Does my book have a higher value to consumers because it took me longer? No, in fact it is often the opposite – the amateur who laboriously spends hours on a product that looks like an amateur creation will be valued less than the product produced by a professional graphic artist and illustrator who is accustomed to working fast and efficiently.

Compare the price of your book with the price of books that have similar size, style, and content. Sales will be hampered if you price above your competition, or high enough that people have to think carefully about the purchase. The lowest price you can charge for your book (with no profit) is $3.59, or $5.30 if you have expanded distribution enabled. You can use ultra low prices as a way to gain consumer interest and reviews, but if you raise the price and sales dry up, you might have given away books to fans who would have otherwise purchased your book.

I've found little to no difference in my sales numbers when I changed the price of my books between $6.99 and $9.99. $10 seems to be the cut off line for impulse buys, and a lower price within the $5-10 range has a minimal effect on sales. Below $5 you get increased sales but lower royalties. You could use this to your advantage in order to get increases sales rank and book reviews, offsetting income generation to a later time.

However it is possible to sell more and make less. Above $12 consumers want more content or better quality paper and that may both inhibit sales and generate low reviews as buyers complain about CreateSpace quality. But your mileage may vary.

CreateSpace allows you to adjust the price of your book at any time. It usually takes an hour or two for Amazon.com to update. You can use this to test out different price points to see what works for you. Just be careful not to read too much into variations in purchases when dealing with a small sample. Unless you're selling 200+ books a day, you will need to retain a price point for a week or two in order to compare. Additionally, because sales are going to vary just based on month and time of year, you should be wary of seasonal demands skewing results.

Your Book's Price on Amazon

The list price you use for your book at CreateSpace may not be the price Amazon offers consumers.

Amazon has complete discretion to increase or decrease the price as it sees fit. Due to dynamic pricing, Amazon may adjust the price of your book multiple times a day. Usually your book will not sell for more than list price, and may be sold at a discount.

My book was originally listed at $8.99. Amazon sold it for $8.99 for 4 days before discounting it by $0.90. 3 days later, they dropped the price to $7.19. Two weeks later, as sales increased, the price bounced around but trended upwards.

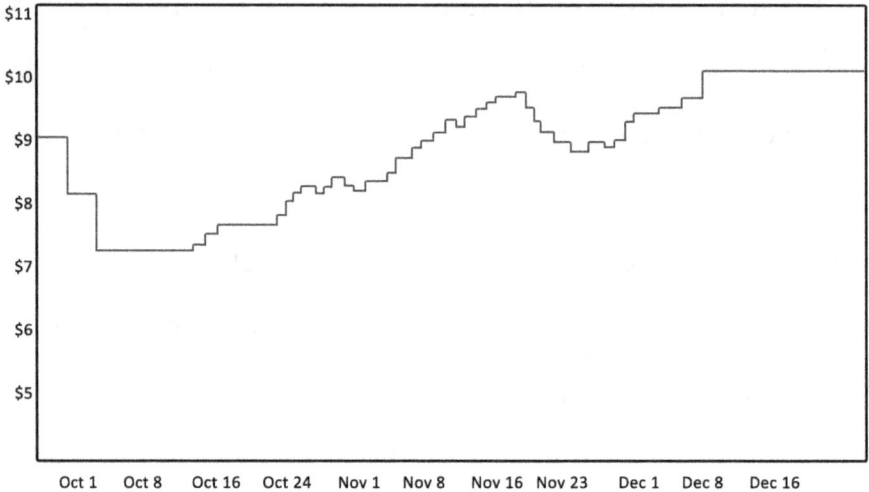

You can use price history trackers such as PriceZombie.com and Keepa.com to track historical movement in your book's selling price as well as sales rank.

Regardless of what Amazon sells your book for, your royalty will be based on your list price. Thus if I list my book at $9.99 (with a $3.84 royalty) and Amazon sells it for $6.99, I still get the full $3.84.

Amazon has mathematical equations in their systems that decide if they want to help push low movement books, or books with a lot of sales, to give better value to their customers. You can't change their algorithm, but you can play with your list price to see what Amazon does in response. Sometimes a change in list price will result in a change with Amazon's pricing. Other times, you can change your list price all you want, and Amazon will retain the current price. For example, my book was selling at $9.99 and I wanted to discount it by $2 to help spur sales. I dropped the price and Amazon continued to sell at $9.99. I dropped the list price further, and still no change.

So I went the other direction and raised my price to $11.99 to see if they'd respond. Amazon still refused to change the price – my book continued to have a $9.99 price tag, but it said "17% off" and showed my list price of $11.99. The nice thing was, raising my price increased my royalties while maintaining the same price for buyers.

The chart below shows my list price (dotted line) vs Amazon's price for my book (solid line).

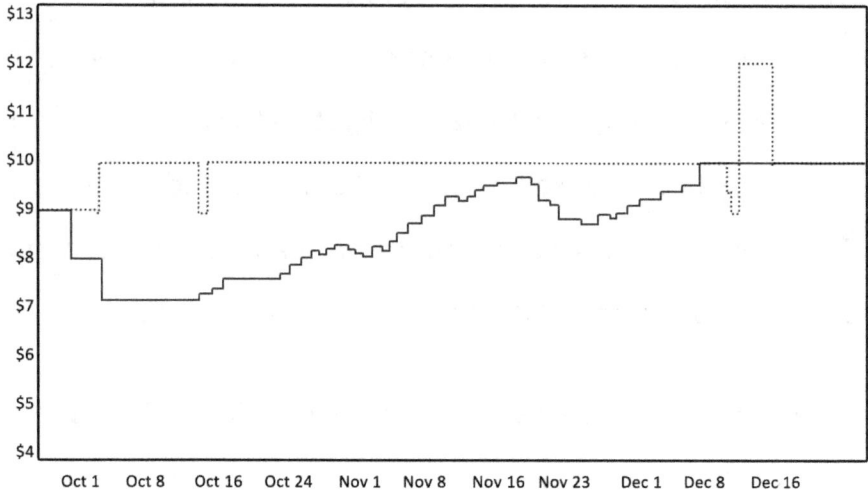

While raising my list price resulted in higher royalties to me, it also runs the very real risk of Amazon eventually moving the price up to $11.99, which would severely hamper sales. Given that I couldn't get Amazon to drop my price earlier, I might be stuck at $11.99! Being the Nervous Nellie that I am, I had visions of my sales dropping through the floor and lowered sales rank booting me out of my chosen categories! I am now very cautious experimenting with prices.

Expanded Distribution

Expanded distribution used to be available to authors at an extra cost, but Amazon now includes it free of charge. Expanded distribution will make your book available to bookstores and other online retailers, expanding the sales potential for your book.

According to the Author's Guild, *"Many books will never find their audience unless they're displayed on bookstore shelves and tables. These books include, of course, children's picture books, art books, and many cookbooks, which have to be seen and held to be appreciated. Bookstores are also destinations for readers, in a way that no online store can replicate. No one plans to take their kids to Amazon on Saturday to browse and pick out a book, for example, and people don't escape to Amazon to unplug and relax for a while. Those trips matter. Marketing studies confirm that readers are far more likely to buy unknown books by unfamiliar authors if they see them in a bookstore. Amazon, on the other hand, excels as a search engine for books readers have already heard of. This is one of the reasons the online market skews heavily toward familiar authors."*

If you aren't a "familiar author" then you want to get into bookstores. If you are a familiar author, then you want to get into bookstores. Either way, the ability to hold your book in hand in a brick and mortar store will drive up your Amazon sales, because Amazon often discounts the price of our books below bookstore costs.

CreateSpace's expanded distribution has lower royalties for you, the author. If you were selling a book at $9.99 with $3.84 in royalties for a sale on Amazon.com, a sale through expanded distribution would give you only 48% of that figure – just $1.84. This is largely due to the fact that expanded distribution is wholesale pricing for retail sales, and thus your book is being sold at a 60% discount on the list price, that comes from both Amazon and the author's cut. On the good side - if a book store is buying up your books, they are buying large quantities and displaying them in-store, which means extra eyes and publicity for your book that drives up Amazon sales as well as those additional bookstore purchases. I would gladly gain that in trade for 60% less profit. However, CreateSpace does not follow the same return and damaged goods practices wholesale buyers are accustomed to when dealing with traditional publishers, and their printing process is not so exact as to be able to accurately print titles on the spines of books with fewer than 120 pages, which bookstores like for display purposes, so bookstores tend to avoid carrying CreateSpace books.

You will likely find most of your expanded distribution sales will go to a company called Book Depository, which is another company Amazon owns. Book Depository provides free worldwide shipping to over 160 countries, and will allow customers to buy your book overseas at lower cost than buying from Amazon.com

Expanded distribution alternatives

You don't need to use CreateSpace's expanded distribution – a simple method to use a different POD service for non-Amazon sales is to print via CreateSpace with Expanded Distribution disabled. Then publish the same book through a different POD publisher, such as IngramSpark, and use them to distribute to brick and mortar stores. IngramSpark has options to allow for book returns, and they also allow you to set the retail discount – 40 to 55%. This gives you a lot more flexibility. There is a major drawback to doing this: cost.

IngramSpark has a yearly fee per title, as well as a fee to create the listing and a fee to make modifications to a listing. Additionally their costs are higher than CreateSpace's, meaning that you will have greater royalties on CreateSpace when IngramSpark's retail discount is set to the same price.

Here are some real world numbers:

Service	List Price	Retail Discount	Royalty Per Book
CreateSpace	$9.99	60%	$1.84
IngramSpark	$9.99	55%	$1.26

While CreateSpace has zero fees, IngramSpark has a $50 setup fee, a $12 yearly fee per title, and an additional fee to make modifications to the book.

Expanded Distribution Expectations

Pictured below is a 2 month breakdown of my sales in CreateSpace based on channel. When I enabled expanded distribution, I had no idea what to expect. I show you my numbers so you might get some idea what it might do for you. I can now see it is a fraction of my Amazon sales, but my product is available to consumers who might have otherwise been unable to purchase.

Sales Channel	Units
	3,783
Amazon	3,625
Expanded Distribution	158

Proof

Once you are done making your cover and interior pages, upload them to CreateSpace, and submit them for review. CreateSpace will usually approve or deny your work within 24 hours. The review process does not check content for typos and errors, nor does it look at your designs. The review process is to make sure that the author specified in your book settings matches the author listed on the cover and on the interior of the book, the ISBN and titles match, and technical issues such as the resolution of the graphics are appropriate. In the event your book is rejected, they will note the reason why, and you can make the required changes and submit again.

When your book is approved, CreateSpace will allow you to see the book in final form (proof) digitally online, and you can order a copy in physical printed form. For your first few books, I recommend reviewing the digital proof until satisfied, and then ordering a physical proof – you will be able to order your book for about $6 shipped. It will take around 1 to 1 ½ weeks to arrive, but that can vary greatly according to demand on CS print shops. I've seen the physical proof arrive faster than their estimate, but I've also seen it arrive 2 weeks late. CreateSpace offers expedited shipping, but the delay in getting the proof is typically due to Amazon orders taking precedence, not transit time. As such, I do not feel that expedited shipping is worth the cost. When the proof arrives, flip through the pages and verify no outstanding issues exist with your graphics and be sure to proof read very carefully. Due to variations of the printing process, look to see how the colors on the cover came out – for example, sometimes blue can come out purple. Look to make sure no text is too close to the edges of the book and have been truncated.

The digital proof will be in the form of a downloadable PDF. CreateSpace will use this PDF to print your book, so it is an accurate representation of what will be printed. CreateSpace also offers a web browser based viewer that renders the cover of the book in addition to the interior. Once you are familiar with CS printing, you can feel confident approving the digital copy without waiting to order the physical copy.

If you spot a problem with either style proof, just upload a new cover or interior and repeat this process. If no problems are seen, approve the proof and your book will be listed on Amazon.

Congratulations, you are now a published author =)

Timeframes

Once you approve the proof, your book will go live. Here are the approximate times for events to occur:

Book to appear on Amazon.com	2-5 hours
Book to appear on Amazon.ca*	7-14 days
Book to appear on Amazon's European regions	3-5 days
Look Inside The Book feature to become active	2-3 weeks

*Amazon claims 30 days, but I've never seen it take that long.

PUBLISHING ELSEWHERE

While this is a book about how to publish on Amazon's CreateSpace, we shouldn't forget that there are alternative routes for you to publish your book. Exploring these options will show you why I feel CreateSpace is the most logical option for self published coloring books.

Traditional publishers

There are a lot of traditional publishers.

You will get more options with a traditional publisher. You can get card stock and perforated paper for interior pages, metallic inks on the cover, and custom sizes. Brick and mortar book stores prefer to do business with well known publishing houses.

But, there's a reason POD publishers are quickly taking over the publishing business – traditional publishers take the lion's size share of the book's profits.

You'd expect an experienced publishing house would do an stellar job when it comes to something that is not within most artist's skill set, and that is marketing your coloring book. Unfortunately, that is not always the case. I've spoken to several authors who chose traditional publishers and haven't been happy with the result.

The publisher sat on their book, expecting the author to do the marketing. If that's the case, then you may get a better quality book, but you also have the enormous and expensive responsibility for driving sales to Amazon and other online venues, as well as brick and mortar stores. All for significantly less royalties than you'll receive through CreateSpace.

Traditional publishers may contact you as an artist for a "work for hire" project, which means they will pay you for your art, but the publisher will hold the copyright and right to reproduce the art on any and all products they choose.

Of course, if your work is of such caliber that publishers are knocking down your door – such as the handful of artists who now sell millions of copies of every book they produce - then you can negotiate a much better deal.

Self Publishing

The two drawbacks of CreateSpace are the paper thickness and interior print quality. Using single sided prints, and vector artwork, you can eliminate most of those issues, but other self publishing solutions can take it a step further – allowing you to pick your own paper, binding, perforated pages, and sell your book to major retailers.

You can buy an inkjet printer and spiral binding machine so you can print all your pages on high quality stock and bind them in a flip book format. Many people sell "artists editions", digital downloads, and prints on Etsy, Ebay, and other artist's venues – even on Amazon.

Small print shops will do all of the above for you and even offer more professional printing options. However, it almost always requires a large up-front investment, as the larger the run the lower the price is per-book. A run of 100 may be $4 per book while a run of 1,000 only $2 per book.

But that also means you have to pay $2,000 when those 1,000 books are delivered to your doorstep.

My main issue with direct sales is most of my time will be spent supervising production, listing the product, dealing with customer service issues such as questions, payments, returns, damaged goods, packing and shipping – all the things that CreateSpace would handle for me. This takes me away from producing art for more coloring books.

If you're interested in selling your self published books on Amazon, you can learn more here: https://services.amazon.com/

You can sell either as FBA (fulfillment by Amazon), which means you send your books to Amazon and they ship out your product, or MF (merchant fulfilled) where you list your books on Amazon, but you are responsible for shipping direct to the customer.

Selling on Amazon is a massive topic all on its own, and is beyond the scope of this book.

COPYRIGHT YOUR WORK

Once your book has been uploaded to CreateSpace, but before you click final approval so it appears live on Amazon, you can download the approved digital proof of your book which contains your book's ISBN and the current date and use it to file your copyright with the US government.

I'm sure you've heard that all artwork is automatically copyrighted at the time of creation, and that you're protected from infringement by others. This is true, but without registering your artwork with the copyright office, you are limited to the infringer's profits as damages (whatever money they made), and you cannot ask for statutory damages for willful infringement. You also can't ask for attorney fees. This means the odds of you obtaining a lawyer willing to take on your infringement case is drastically lower if your work isn't registered.

The best way to protect your work is to file before your work is published. That creates a benchmark date that is used in legal filings. If your work has already been published, you can still file up to 3 months later. It costs $55, and you can submit your book's information online.

Create an account on http://copyright.gov/eco/ and it will walk you through the entire process. The only thing that threw me for a loop my first time filing: I was not able to find where to submit my artwork in the online forms. It turns out that you don't get to submit the artwork until after you've submitted your book information and paid the filing fees.

The entire process to copyright your book should only take about 10-20 minutes.

AMAZON BEST SELLERS RANK

Amazon's Best Sellers Rank (BSR), also known as sales rank (SR), describes how well a product is selling on Amazon relative to other products within the same upper category. This innocuous term has massive implications when selling on Amazon.

To more clearly illustrate what sales rank means, the very best sales rank is 1. If your book had a sales rank of 1 in the category Books, that means out of all the books on Amazon, your book is selling the most. A sales rank of 2 means it is the second best selling book.

BSR is relative to other books. Lets say you were selling 100 books a day, and suddenly you were selling 200 in a day. If you ranked at 1,000 in books and everyone else also doubled their sales, your BSR would stay exactly the same.

Since sales rank is relative to other products within a category, and sales will vary due to time of year, you cannot use it to accurately determine sales numbers. But knowledgeable people can make an educated guess. For example, if you are selling 80 books a day in April, your sales rank may be 2,000. In December, due to the massive number of new releases competing for Christmas shoppers and increased sales, those same 80 books a day might show a sales rank closer to 5,000.

The details to the algorithm behind Amazon's sales rank is not publicly disclosed. Based on monitoring my own book's rankings it appears that sales rank is weighted heavily towards the latest 7 days of sales. Meaning that on the 8th day, a poor sales day rolls out of the 7 day period, and the sales rank may improve because of it. The closer to the top you are, the more sales you need to move up. If you have a sales rank of 2,500 it may take 10 more sales every day for 7 days to move to 2,300. But if you are closer to the bottom of all sellers you can see dramatic moves with just one sale. Typically a book that has a BSR of 1,000,000 (rarely selling) can move to 600,000 BSR from a single sale. Then 2 weeks later a second sale may boost it up to 400,000.

Best sellers rank also matters when it comes to subcategories. The #1 book in a subcategory is not likely to be #1 in the top category of Books, but BSR within subcategories can vary significantly. With a BSR of 1,500 (in Books), I was #2 in Children's Coloring Books and #42 in Coloring Books for Grownups. When my BSR dropped to 4,192, I moved to the #4 spot in Children's Coloring Books and was completely bounced out of the top 100 (I was #124) for Coloring Books for Grownups. The Children's Coloring Books category is more competitive and there were a lot more books between 1,500 and 4,100.

Sales made through CreateSpace or through expanded distribution do not count towards your BSR. Only purchases made through Amazon factor towards your BSR.

BOOK CATEGORY ON AMAZON

When you filled in your book's details on CreateSpace, one of the questions was to define your BISAC category. This selection will automatically place your book in one Amazon category, and an Amazon representative may manually add it into 2 additional. Due to the manual intervention, coloring books often find themselves added to nonsense categories such as Humor by a representative who doesn't understand the book's content. The good news is, you can request changes or additional categories if you have less than three.

Why category is important

Books are ranked within a category based on Sales Rank. You should pick categories that are relevant to your book's category (such as coloring books for grown ups), and content (for example, meditation or colored pencil), but also categories where you feel confident you will be able to quickly rank in the top 100.

Being listed in the top 100 for a category means you will appear in the "Best Sellers", "Hot New Releases", "Most Wished For" and "Gift Ideas" for the category. If you are not in the top 100 you do not appear in any list that pulls from that category.

To figure out the sales rank needed to appear in a category, simply browse to a category, click to the last page of the list, and look at the 100th book.

In the example below, you can see the 3 categories I selected, and where my book ranks. We can see that only 1 out of the 3 categories are currently providing traffic to the book:

Amazon Best Sellers Rank: #4,528 in Books (See Top 100 in Books)
      #4 in Books > Children's Books > Activities, Crafts & Games > Activity Books > **Coloring Books**
      #129 in Books > Arts & Photography > Drawing > **Coloring Books for Grown-Ups**
      #181 in Books > Crafts, Hobbies & Home > **Crafts & Hobbies**

A quick way to find categories that might fit your book: search Amazon for similar books, then look at what categories they are listed in. You will find that books are listed in a wide variety of categories, many of which I'd have never thought of.

Changing the Category

Changing categories is a manual process. You'll have to use this form and ask a customer service rep to make the change:

https://authorcentral.amazon.com/gp/help/contact-us

Select "My Books" > "Update information about a book" > "Browse Categories"

LOOK INSIDE THE BOOK

Amazon's "Look Inside The Book" (LITB) is a feature that shows off the interior of your book. This feature is automatically available to all CreateSpace books, but will take several weeks to be functional for new books. By default, it will list only a few pages, and typically focuses on pages with text.

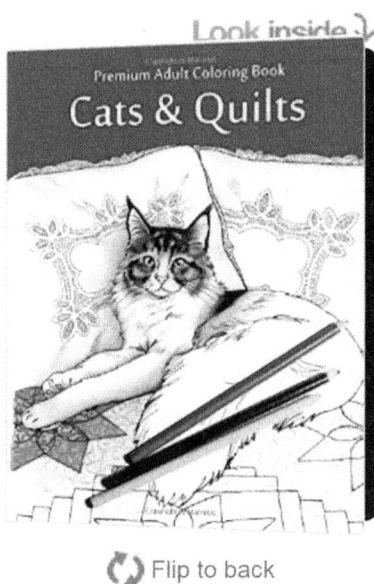

If you'd like to ask Amazon to change the percent of your book that is available to the Look Inside The Book (LITB), email:

insidethebook-submission@amazon.com

and give them the URL to your book and the % you'd like. Use increments of 10%.

I normally use 20 - 40% for my books. Keep in mind that LITB will be showing users a 600 x 776 sized copy of your illustrations, so if you are worried about users getting a free copy of your book, don't enable 100% for LITB! I have personally seen people sharing LITB images on Pintrest and FaceBook groups. They are easily spotted due to the *"Copyright Material"* watermark at the top and bottom of each image.

MARKETING

Creating and publishing your coloring book is only the beginning. Marketing your book is vital to success. No matter how good your book is, if no one knows about it, no one will buy it.

The skill set required to create a book does not often include marketing savvy. If you publish under CreateSpace or other POD publishing sources, you accept the fact that you must do all of the marketing.

Read that again. You must do ALL of the marketing.

Marketing your book will require a lot of effort and time. At least as much time, and possibly more, as making your book.

It is not unusual for family members to tackle the marketing job in order to keep the artist making more art.

The following is a list of the more common techniques used to market a coloring book.

Product Page

Your book's listing on Amazon is the primary vehicle for sales. In order to move books, your book's page should have plenty of positive reviews, especially reviews containing photos of colored pages from your book and or video reviews.

Who better to make such a review than the author themselves, or at least friends and family, maybe even another coloring book author, who can be depended to sing our praise and present our book in its best light. Not so fast!

Amazon states this about customer reviews:

> *"If you have a direct or indirect financial interest in a product, or perceived to have a close personal relationship with its author or artist, we'll likely remove your review. We don't allow authors to submit customer reviews on their own books even when they disclose their identity."*

They specifically state this type of review is not permitted:

> *"An artist posts a positive review on a peer's album in exchange for receiving a positive review from them"*

Amazon is excellent at data mining. If you have your Facebook account linked to your Amazon account, they have access to your friends list and can identify possible conflicts of interest.

Fortunately, there are top Amazon reviewers who purchase an amazing amount of books and give accurate reviews, complete with videos and pictures. Often, their contact email address is listed directly in their public Amazon account.

Many authors include a paragraph on the last page asking purchasers to leave a review if they like the book, and you can certainly ask on your website or in your mailing list for satisfied buyers to leave reviews.

Boosting Sales Rank

Amazon prohibits inflating sales rank for sellers. In the case of your own books, you aren't the seller, CreateSpace is. So a sale is a sale. Thus you can buy your own book at full price, and it will help your sales rank. Due to the cost, I don't recommend buying many of your own book, but you can use it to get a small boost when starting out. I combine my own purchases with giveaways, so I get a double exposure (the give away, and the sales rank boost) for the same cash outlay.

Author Page

Once your book is published and selling on Amazon's website, you'll be able to visit Author Central and login with your normal Amazon account and claim your book. At the top of your book's page on Amazon they list your name as the author, hot linked to your dedicated author page. Author Central allows you to add content to this page.

Users can then subscribe for updates and they can monitor the page for activity. In addition to listing your currently available books, it lets you upload video files, and can automatically import your blog and twitter posts. This is where you can post your reviews and promote your other books.

Author Central will also allow you to override your CreateSpace defaults for your book. Meaning, you can change your book's description directly on Author Central.

WARNING: If you modify your book's description through Author Central, you will have to remember to return to Author Central for future changes, as the updates you make on CreateSpace will no longer publish to your Amazon listings! This is important because CreateSpace book description allows html color tags to your text, whereas Author Central strips those tags out. Thus if you use Author Central, you will not be able to change the font color of your book description.

Preorders

Preorder means placing an order for a book not yet available. A book sale counts towards sales rank only when the book has sold, thus preorders do not count towards sales rank. However, the moment the book goes on sale, all preorders are converted into sales at the same time. What this means is that a book with a preorder can go from no sales rank to a very good sales rank in an instant. Thus a preorder of 100 books could make a book instantly rank at 2,000 BSR (or better). A book released without a preorder, selling the same 100 books over the course of a week would rank about 4 times poorer in sales rank. That initial boost would gain visibility in search results and within the categories that could help sustain sales.

Now that I've told you how great preorders are, I have bad news to report: CreateSpace has no option for you to do a preorder.

There is a way to trick CreateSpace into what amounts to a preorder, but it could easily blow up in your face. To do it, you will have to create an Amazon seller account, create a new product listing for your book, and create a preorder for your book.

When it is time for you to convert the preorders to sales, you'll have to contact CreateSpace, and have a representative manually swap the preorder book listing with your CreateSpace book listing. This is NOT a normal procedure. Most representatives will not know what to do or how to do it properly. If the representative messes up the swap, all preorders will be canceled and lost forever.

The reason why I do not recommend doing preorders using this method is that CreateSpace representatives are hit or miss. Some are knowledgeable and do a great job, but the majority I've dealt with do not seem to care. I have made many calls to CreateSpace where the representative has claimed they'd update or modify my book's listing as requested, only for me to find out a week later that the representative never actually made the requested modifications. To this end, I think a CreateSpace preorder is more likely to end in frustration than not.

Black Hat SEO

This refers to the use of aggressive techniques to trick search engines into ranking something higher than it should. SEO stands for Search Engine Optimization.

This section is to alert you to what others are doing and to draw attention to the issue for sake of completeness of this book.

I do NOT encourage the use of black hat SEO tactics as they diminish the end user experience – something Amazon is steadfastly against. While tricks like keyword stuffing may work now, the more widely such tactics are (ab)used the less useful Amazon's search becomes. Amazon will sooner or later tire of this and address the issue. It will be anyone's guess what remedy they take, but Amazon is known to delete accounts and withhold royalties if their terms of service are broken.

A simple example of black hat SEO would be keyword stuffing, which is writing a title or description for a website or product, and repeatedly mentioning targeted keywords.

Here is a real example from the bottom of a description of a book on Amazon that at one time ranked #1 in books:

"TAGS: adult coloring books best sellers, coloring books for adults relaxation, artists illustrators, mandalas, stress relieving patterns, coloring pages for adults, meditation, mindfulness meditation, nature mandalas coloring books for grownups, anti-stress management, Sweary Words coloring book ,swear coloring book, cursing coloring book, sweary words coloring book, the sweary coloring book, sweary coloring book, swearing coloring book , swear word coloring book"

Keyword stuffing is a black hat SEO technique that worked in the early days of web search engines – by repeating the targeted word multiple times on a webpage, the simple text matching algorithm assumed the website had a lot to say about the topic and thus boosted its ranking for searches on those terms. These days search engines like Google can tell if a page is keyword stuffing, and excessive use of a keyword can actually be a deterrent.

Authors are currently putting keywords into the author field for their book. This is done because a search that matches an author's name will make the author's books appear. So if the author's name is "Sweary coloring book", the book's title is "Sweary coloring book", and that keyword is repeated in the description, the Amazon search engine thinks it's a really good match when someone searches for those words. I've spoken with Amazon about this issue and they tell me they are actively looking into the problem and a resolution is forthcoming.

This is what Amazon says:

> *"Don't provide inaccurate, misleading, or irrelevant information such as competitor product, brand or author name, wrong gender, etc. Providing misleading or irrelevant information is against Amazon policy; your listing will be removed and your account will be suspended."*

http://www.amazon.com/gp/help/customer/display.
html/?nodeId=201991750

While the quote is specific for seller accounts and not book authors, it shows how serious the issue it is to Amazon. They will immediately suspend an account over it. Getting a closed account reopened will take weeks and they are not often forgiving.

Facebook Groups

You might not know it, but Facebook lets you chat and share things with more than just your relatives and friends. Facebook has discussion groups too, and there are many coloring book specific groups available.

Since the group names can change, and what is popular may vary, rather than listing the groups I currently use, here is a FaceBook search:

https://www.facebook.com/search/groups/?q=coloring%20book

There are dozens of groups, some with over 40,000 members. This is a massive audience that you can reach at zero cost to you.

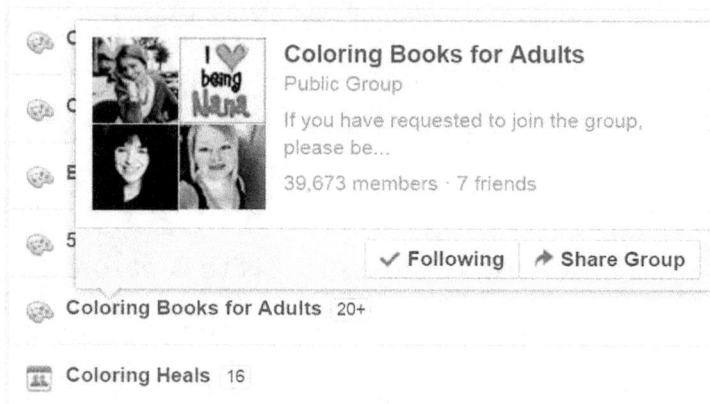

Coloring Books for Adults
Public Group

If you have requested to join the group, please be...

39,673 members · 7 friends

✓ Following ↗ Share Group

Coloring Books for Adults 20+

Coloring Heals 16

Each group is run by different individuals with different rules. Read the rules and contact an admin to introduce yourself. Authors and artists are usually welcome additions to any group as long as announcements about a book and links to a Amazon page are made within reason. You don't want to get a reputation for being a spammer! Make time to participate in the group. Don't just advertise your book and leave. Answer questions, participate in contests and giveaways, create a different album for each group, offer free coloring pages, post colored-in pages and praise those who have taken the time and effort to bring your b&w creation to life with colors. Colorists enjoy feeling like they have a personal relationship with you – and they should, because they are your fan base and your best customers.

Be warned that many of the larger Facebook groups are run by individuals or companies that have a commercial interest in coloring books. Be it a website with affiliate links to coloring books, or publishing their own books that you will compete with. Not to worry – in the quest to obtain subscribers, these groups welcome artists as they add content to the group.

One thing I notice other authors doing when they promote their book: They make the same post in all the groups at the same time. I don't do that – I limit myself to posting to 2 or 3 groups per day at a time. Facebook groups have user overlap, which means if a user happens to be on at the time you make the post, they might see it, but most won't. When you post to all groups at the same time, you limit yourself to just those users who are online when your post is visible. By spreading your posts across several days, at different times, and by hitting smaller numbers of groups per day, you increase the odds of a user seeing your post.

Additionally, if your goal is to increase your sales rank, a single day sales spike is not nearly as helpful as elevated sales across an entire week. Your BSR average will be better and not drop off as quickly.

Facebook Page

You can create your own Facebook page that people can "Like".

The page can also link to your personal website if you have one. Use it to share upcoming books, your works in progress (WIP) and more.

Likewise, you could also create a FaceBook group for your business.

Create a Page
Create a Facebook Page to build a closer relationship with your audience and customers.   Pages I Like   Pages I Manage

Local Business or Place   Company, Organization or Institution   Brand or Product

Artist, Band or Public Figure   Entertainment   Cause or Community

Giveaways

A giveaway is where you give away your book in order to gain interest. It works well in conjunction with Facebook groups. It could be as simple as announcing the giveaway, supplying a sample illustration from your book, and saying that in a week the two most up-voted colored illustrations posted will get a free copy of your book. If they don't win, even if they don't participate in the contest, people see your book and might buy a copy or add it to their wish list. It really works well when those users share their artwork with others — so the more colorists who have your artwork and are sharing the result, the more people are exposed to your book and that means more potential sales.

Be careful with contests, there are strict rules that vary based on country. If you do it wrong, you could be breaking the law. Here is a blog post that discusses some of the details:

http://www.socialmediaexaminer.com/social-media-promotions-and-the-law-what-you-need-to-know/

To avoid the hassles I prefer to let group admins run the contest. I purchase the required copies of my book from Amazon (or CreateSpace when dealing with 2 or more books) and have them mailed directly to the group admin, and let them mail the books to the winners. Now I'm not running the giveaway, and have no red tape or laws to worry about.

Personal Website or Blog

When you tell others about your artwork, you could tell them to visit Amazon and search for you by name or by book title, but few will remember. An alternative is to run your own website.

A personal website is a place to present your books and their content in depth. You can add as many videos and preview photos as you want, you can use a website to reach your fans and let them get to know you. Create a mail list, offer free printables, run giveaways and contests, set up a gallery to showcase your fans colored-in pictures.

I do not bother with search engine optimize (SEO) for my website – the process of getting ranked in Google for any useful keyword is a massive undertaking with minimal reward. All roads lead to Amazon, and that is where I put my focus.

A personal website works really well in conjunction with Facebook groups. When people ask where to buy my books, I direct them to my website, and more often than not turn one potential sale into a fan who will make repeat purchases.

Google

At the time of this writing, Amazon has 482,914,032 unique products on their site. Given what we know of Amazon's sales rank, anything beyond the top 20% gets little to no sales movement, and you really want to be in the top 5% for decent sales. Thus only about 24M products are going to be useful to index. Amazon doesn't provide visibility to their entire product index as there is a hard limit on both search and category listings. This means even if Google's crawlers follow every link on the Amazon website, they would not see most of the products Amazon has for sale. If you want your book listed on Amazon to be indexed by Google, linking to your book from your personal website (or any other publicly available website that is crawled by Google) will be the fastest way to get Google to see it.

YouTube

YouTube is an amazing way to promote your book. It can be as simple as aiming a camera at your book and flipping through the pages while explaining your intent and ideas behind the illustrations. This is called an artist's walk through. It fosters a personal relationship with your fans while showing them exactly what is contained in your book.

You can add a link to your book's page on Amazon in the video description on YouTube.

Once you make your walk through video, you can include it on your website, in your Facebook posts, and your author's page on Amazon.

Twitter & Instagram

These are social media sites that let you share information and images with others. If you have the time, you can build up a following and share progress with others on your artwork and sales.

Reddit

Reddit is a giant discussion forum. Topics are called subreddits. Each subreddit is user moderated by whomever started the group. Each subreddit will have its own rules to follow. There isn't a lot of coloring book activity on reddit. /r/coloring is slow. /r/art might work for you, but it will be hit or miss, and users aren't focused on coloring books.

Additionally, users of reddit are against any hint of self promotion, and so posting a link to your book on amazon will likely be viewed as spam. Being able to make a successful post about your coloring book can be done, but it will take the finesse of someone who knows how to appeal to its unique userbase.

My recommendation: Do not to try to directly promote your book.

Share images you've colored from your book, mention the title of the book, but no links to it. If people are interested, they can search for it. If someone asks where you got the image, then you can post a link. This will have far more success than directly advertising.

You can also try your luck at /r/Coloringbookspastime and /r/comics.

Search engine and social media ads

You can pay for ads to obtain traffic to your Facebook page, blog, website, and your Amazon product page. Ads can be purchased from Facebook, Google, Bing, Reddit, and many more.

At this point in time, I cannot recommend running ads to promote the sale of coloring books as it is extremely difficult to get a positive return on investment. Ads will cost anywhere from 6 cents to 2 dollars a click, but more typically in the 30 - 90 cent range. That only gets a visitor to your site – you still have to sell them on the product. Search traffic has average conversion rate of 5.63%. If you were paying 35 cents a click, it would cost you over $6 per book purchase! To put it another way, if you bought 5,000 clicks at 35 cents a click, it would cost you $2,430 for the ads, and your $9.99 book on Amazon would net you $1,078 in royalties.

See what I mean about it being difficult to get a return on investment?

It gets even worse if you are using Facebook ads, as conversions are even harder to obtain.

Local

You don't need to rely strictly on the internet to get interest. You can approach your local newspaper and TV stations to report on a local interest story. Here is an example of someone who did just that:

http://www.ktva.com/coloring-books-for-adults-wasilla-woman-creates-unusual-way-to-unwind-418

Another local route is your library, community center, nursing home, hospital, or place of worship. Offer to host a coloring night where you bring coloring pages and copies of your books.

FAQ

CreateSpace is prompting me to release my coloring book on Kindle, should I do it?

Its against the rules to publish a coloring book on Kindle:

"Books that are not suited for Kindle are removed from sale. Some books are simply not well suited to the Kindle format. These include any kind of book where the main purpose is to allow the reader to write or color on the pages. These books are better suited to publishing in a physical form. Examples of books not suited to the Kindle format include the following:

- *Puzzle books*
- *Blank Journals*
- *Pattern books*
- *Coloring books"*

https://kdp.amazon.com/help?topicId=A1MMQ0JHRBEINX

Rules aside, every coloring book I've seen on Kindle has eventually racked up negative reviews when Kindle owners find out they can't print directly from their Kindle device. People do not read instructions, so even if you have a link to a pdf for their PC, they will complain.

When does a sale appear in the CreateSpace dashboard?

Technically, you do not get paid for a book being sold, you get paid when your book gets printed. This matters because if an Amazon customer buys your book, the book gets printed, then the customer cancels the order before it ships, that printed book will sit in the warehouse till someone else orders the book. This can cause your sales to look skewed or seem off.

I can tell you from past experience, that an Amazon sale can appear in the CS dashboard within 10-20 minutes of the sale, but I've also seen CS orders take much longer.

I'll give you a real life extreme example of how long a sale may be delayed: I released a new book on CreateSpace. It was selling 20 or fewer books per day for the first week. My mother decided she wanted to buy 30 and give them to friends. I have seen her Amazon purchase invoice, so I know she bought my book, yet CreateSpace dashboard did not show any day with 30 or more orders. The day of the sale, the day it was printed, the day it was shipped and the day it was delivered to my mother's house, and the next three days, all showed under 30 orders. How could this be unless Amazon/ CreateSpace was not recording my mother's purchases? As it turns out, about a week after her purchase I went back and saw the day she purchased the books was showing 48 orders instead of 18.

Long story short, orders may not only take a while to appear, but they can appear on days you thought had already been totaled and orders accounted for.

Expanded distribution sales can take a month or longer to appear in the dashboard.

Is there any way to track purchases on CreateSpace to verify purchases are accurately being recorded?

Since Amazon and CreateSpace are handling printing and sales, some people have wondered if all books sold are accounted for. While there is no way for you to independently confirm ordered books are all accounted for, there is a trick you can use to run your own tests.

The trick works on the basis that royalties earned are based on the price of a book. Since you can change the price of your book dynamically, you can thus adjust your royalties earned, and thus independently track sales at specific price points.

List Price	Royalty
$9.99	$3.84
$9.98	$3.83
$9.96	$3.82

Modify your book with a $9.99 list price to sell at $9.98. When the $9.98 price is shown on Amazon.com, you can place an order for the book and change the list price to $9.96. You now know for a fact that your book had at least one sale at that price point, and you must see a corresponding royalty on your CreateSpace dashboard for $3.83. By repeating this process with various price points and asking friends with different Amazon accounts to make a purchase within those windows, you should be able to independently confirm known sales are being correctly reported and put your mind at ease.

Caveat: If the book is actively sold to the general public, you might run into the aforementioned situation of a printed book order being canceled, which can result in a previously printed (but unsold) copy being used to fulfill a later order at a price point at which you purchased. This would cause the expected royalty to not appear in the dashboard. Thus this method will work best for titles with low sales, or for new titles, though over time you should be able to eliminate those unlikely situations from skewing your test results.

When is a good time to launch my new book?

You might think that launching your book as soon as it is available is a good idea, but sometimes it isn't. Lets say you were aiming to complete a book in November, but got derailed for whatever reason and completed the book on Christmas Day. Once you submit the book for approval, order a proof, and confirm everything looks good, it's already January. If you launch your book in January, you might find your sales will suffer no matter what you do. Why? Retail sales slump in January and February. People overloaded their credit cards in December and are not buying nearly as much stuff. A person who is into coloring books probably received coloring books for Christmas. They will have plenty to color and won't be nearly as likely to be hunting for a new title.

Below is the consumer activity level of about a half million Amazon customers from Jan 1 to Dec 31st 2015. It shows that January, February, August, September, October are the 5 slowest months. March, November, and December are the three peaks.

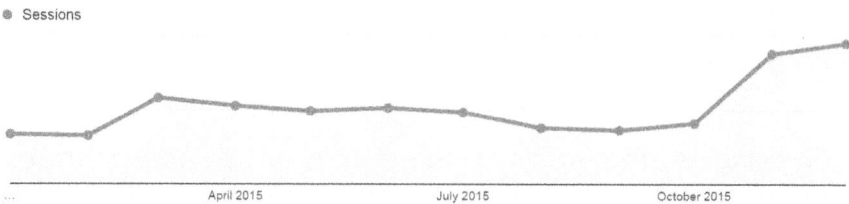

If you want to capitalize on November and December traffic, your new book should published and available to consumers at least 2 months prior. It takes time to acquire reviews and grow sales rank, which will place you in best seller's lists.

I see multiple listings for my book on Amazon, what can I do about it?

Piracy is a serious problem for coloring book artists.

There are people who copy entire books and sell them alongside the real book on Amazon. They create secondary listings with the same information as the original, and hope people buy their copy instead of yours. There are also sellers who list books and create duplicate listings on accident.

Creating duplicate listings is against the Terms of Service for seller accounts:

"Creating duplicate product detail pages: Creating a product detail page for a product already in the Amazon catalog is prohibited.

Creating separate listings: Sellers may not create separate listings for identical copies of the same item. Individually listing the same item several times is confusing for buyers and frustrating for other sellers. Sellers must use the quantity field to offer multiple copies of the same item, and only list separately if offering the same item in different conditions."

https://www.amazon.com/gp/help/customer/display.html?nodeId=200414320

There isn't going to be a way for you to know which is which, so the best thing to do is contact Amazon support and ask them to merge the listings. Then your legitimate CreateSpace book will be the seller with the buy box.

You can use the consumer facing Contact Us page to alert Amazon:

https://www.amazon.com/gp/help/customer/contact-us

Just select "Something else" > "Non-order question" and the representative you speak with will forward the merge request to the correct department.

It will take 1-3 days for the merge to be updated on Amazon.

My book is already published, can I change the contents?

You should have a physical proof made for your first few books, in order for you to see how your artwork converts into print. Once you get the hang of it, you might be able to rely on the online proof. That said, even the best of us will eventually spot a problem after the book has been approved and is being printed for customers.

CreateSpace allows you to unlock an approved book and make changes to both the cover and the interior. Please keep in mind that when you unlock the book, it will be pulled from Amazon and it will not be available for sale till you submit your changes and they are approved. This can potentially bring your book offline for several days, damaging your sales rank, and costing you sales not only during the downtime, but also in the future as it will take time to recover rank.

My book received a negative review. Can I get it removed?

Reviews can only be removed if they break the review creation guidelines, which can be found here:

http://www.amazon.com/gp/help/customer/display.html?nodeId=201602680

If the review is profane, has personal info (such as phone numbers or addresses), non Amazon URLs, hate speech, or promotes illegal activities, it can be removed. Reviews may also be removed if the review isn't about the book itself, but about things such as packaging and shipping.

If you spot a review that you think might break the review creation guidelines, you can click the "Report abuse" link next to the review and explain what rule the review broke. This will create a case with the review team. You can also go through Author Central > "Contact Us" > "Call Me", and they can open a case for you. Cases may take up to 48 hours to be reviewed.

REFERENCE ILLUSTRATIONS

The following illustrations may be used as references to see how various printing methods appear in printed form. Some file formats will work better than others, some illustrations will print better than others.

CreateSpace's printing process will internally raster all images during the printing process, but you will still see a difference between raster and vector submitted images.

You will find that vector images with pure black lines will have the best print results on CreateSpace. Resolutions greater than 300 dpi currently do not improve print quality. Lines that are not pure black will contain visible halftones and thus should be avoided when possible.

Raster

RGB 600 dpi illustration in png format

This is an image as it came directly out of the scanner.
Due to not adjusting the levels on the illustration, you should
see light halftones across the skin, instead of pure white.
This will make the image look "muddy" instead of clean.

Also note that the black areas on the dress are made up of many
tiny black dots instead of solid black. This is because the blacks
on this image are not pure black.

Raster

Grayscale 600 dpi illustration in png format

This is the same image as on the previous page, but converted to grayscale instead of RGB.

It should look very similar.

Raster

Grayscale 300 dpi scan in png format

300 dpi version of the illustration on the previous page
so you can see how it compares to the 600 dpi versions.

You should not see any significant differences.

Raster

Grayscale 600 dpi raw scan in jpg format.

This is the same as the 600 dpi grayscale image on page 127, but saved in jpg format instead of png, which is a lossy file format. It should look about the same to the naked eye.

Vector

Adobe Illustrator's "image trace" exported in eps format

This is the result of converting a raster image to vector by use of "image trace". All lines are pure black, all white areas are pure white. There are no visible halftones anywhere on the page. The blacks in the dress should be solid without any screening.

This should result in the best printed lines CreateSpace can produce.

Vector

Vector Magic exported in eps format

This is the result of converting a raster image to vector, by use of Vector Magic software, then saved in a vector format.

Like the Adobe Illustrator example on the previous page, this should produce the best quality lines CreateSpace can print.

You can use this example to get an idea of the differences between Adobe Illustrator's "image trace" and Vector Magic's output. Inkscape is a free alternative that can produce similar results.

Raster

Grayscale 600 dpi image converted to vector then exported in png format for printing

This is the result of converting the vector image on page 135 back into raster. Normally you would not convert vector back to raster, but in case you did, the results would still be fairly clean.

To the naked eye, this should look as clean as it did in vector format. However closer examination using a magnifying glass on the roots of her hair will show jagged edges not seen on the vector version. For the most part, this print quality is acceptable and consumers will not notice or complain.

Raster

Grayscale 1,200 dpi in png format

This is the result of converting a vector image into a 1,200 dpi raster image. The purpose of this is to show how 1,200 dpi compares to the 300 and 600 previously shown.

You should not see any improvement compared to the 300 dpi print because that is the maximum quality CreateSpace can print.

ANY QUESTIONS?

Do you have a question for a topic I didn't cover? Not to worry, you can join the Coloring Book Author Support on Facebook and get live help from hundreds of CreateSpace authors:

https://www.Facebook.com/groups/ColoringBookAuthorSupport/

www.ingramcontent.com/pod-product-compliance
Lightning Source LLC
LaVergne TN
LVHW051415080426
835508LV00022B/3099